# 101 Windows Tips & Tricks

Scott Dunn • Charles Bermant • Jesse Berst

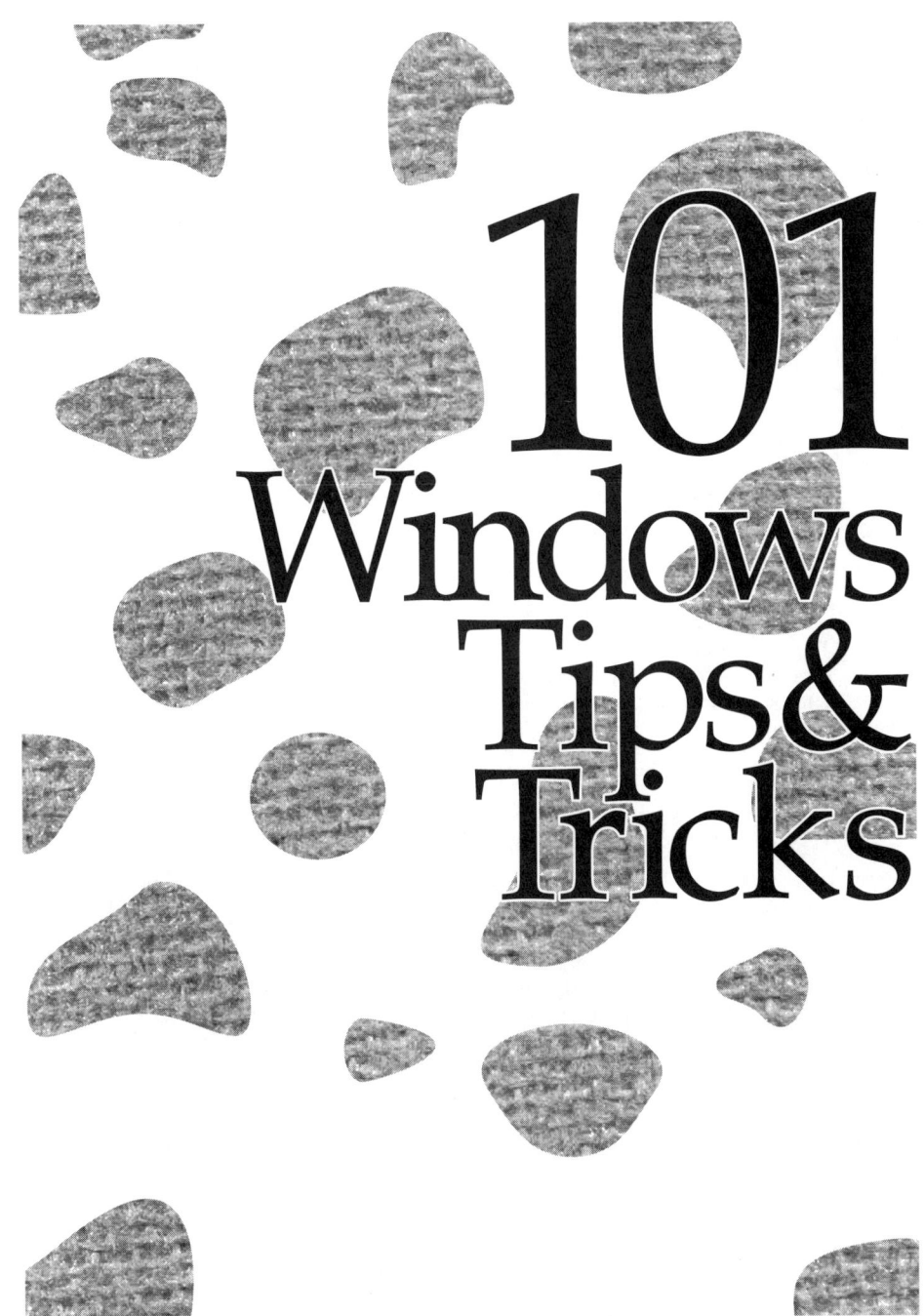

# 101 Windows Tips & Tricks

**Scott Dunn • Charles Bermant • Jesse Berst**

101 Windows Tips & Tricks
Scott Dunn, Charles Bermant, and Jesse Berst

PEACHPIT PRESS, INC.
2414 Sixth St.
Berkeley, CA 94710
(800) 283-9444
(510) 548-4393
(510) 548-5991 (fax)

Copyright (c) 1992 Scott Dunn, Charles Bermant, and Jesse Berst
Cover design by Ted Mader + Associates
Interior design by Scott Dunn, Tim Toyoshima, and Byron Canfield
Illustration by Scott Dunn and Byron Canfield
Production by Byron Canfield

All rights reserved. No part of this book may be reproduced or transmitted in any form or by any means, electronic, mechanical, photocopying, recording, or otherwise, without the prior written permission of the publisher. For information, contact Peachpit Press.

NOTICE OF LIABILITY:
The information in this book is distributed on an "As is" basis, without warranty. While every precaution has been taken in the preparation of this book neither the author nor Peachpit Press, Inc., shall have any liability to any person or entity with respect to any liability, loss, or damage caused or alleged to be caused directly or indirectly by the instructions contained in this book or by the computer software and hardware products described herein.

TRADEMARKS:
Throughout this book, trademarked names are used. Rather than but a trademark symbol in every occurrence of a trademarked name, we are using the names only in an editorial fashion and to the benefit of the trademark owner, with no intention of infringement of the trademark. Where those designations appear in this book, the designations have been printed in initial caps.

ISBN 0-938151-55-X

0 9 8 7 6 5 4 3 2 1

Printed and bound in the United States of America

"For my lover, David."
— Scott

"For Jill, without whom I would still be impossible."
— Charles

"Dedicated to Ted Nace, everyone's favorite computer publisher."
— Jesse

# Acknowledgements

Besides the authors themselves, several people were an essential part of getting this book to you:

John Hedtke did editing and supplied additional material on telecommunications and games. John is the award-winning author of half a dozen best-selling computer books including *Using Computer Bulletin Boards* and *Winning! The Awesome and Amazing Insider's Book of Windows Game Tips, Traps, and Sneaky Tricks*.

Anne Edmondson provided editorial support. Byron Canfield, Seattle's Ventura wizard, did the layout. Tim Toyoshima worked with Scott Dunn to create the design.

Third-party software mentioned in this book was graciously supplied by the manufacturers.

Our thanks to John, Byron, Anne, and Tim, along with others too numerous to mention.

# CONTENTS

Introduction ................................................................................. 1

**CHAPTER 1:** **BLAST OFF** ............................................................... 3
*Launching, managing, and closing Windows applications*
Getting with the Program and File Managers .................... 4
Lifting Off ........................................................................... 13
When Your Heart Belongs to Data ..................................... 26
Making a Soft Landing ....................................................... 32
Summing Up ....................................................................... 36

**CHAPTER 2:** **DOING DOS** ............................................................. 37
*Achieving maximum cooperation from non-Windows applications*
PIF the Magic DOS Gun ...................................................... 39
Parameter Power ................................................................ 44
Down Memory Lane ........................................................... 48
DOS Dos and Don'ts ........................................................... 54
Summing Up ....................................................................... 59

**CHAPTER 3:** **PRINTS CHARMING** ............................................. 61
*Simplifying printing and font handling*
A-Fonting We Will Go ........................................................ 62
Printing to Disk .................................................................. 73
Particularly PostScript ....................................................... 78
A Miscellany of Speed Tips ............................................... 84
Summing Up ....................................................................... 88

**CHAPTER 4:** **OPTIMIZING YOUR SYSTEM** .......................... 89
*Managing memory, disk space, and resources for maximum power*

Jogging the Memory ............................................................ 90
Driving that Disk .................................................................. 98
Take It on the Road ........................................................... 103
The Thrill of Acceleration ................................................. 107
The Agony of Defeat .......................................................... 113
All the Right Moves ........................................................... 118
Summing Up ...................................................................... 126

**CHAPTER 5:** **CUSTOM MADE WINDOWS** ........................... 127
*Tweaking your system for maximum convenience and delight*

WIN.INI is Everything ....................................................... 128
Dress for Success .............................................................. 134
Gimme Shell-ter ................................................................ 141
Hue and Cry ....................................................................... 147
Icon Get No Satisfaction .................................................. 153
Summing Up ...................................................................... 157

**CHAPTER 6:** **FUN AND FUNCTIONAL** ................................. 159
*A miscellany of utilities and tricks*

Baby Steps ......................................................................... 160
Control Boxing .................................................................. 172
Window Boxing ................................................................. 179
And Now, the Moment You've All Been Waiting For ......... 186
Summing Up ...................................................................... 198

# Introduction

Dear Reader:

You are holding in your hands one of the finest collections of Windows information known to humankind. Not only has this book been assembled at great and incalculable expense, not only have dozens of experts spent years in its development, not only has the book been carried across the burning sands and the seven seas to get it to the stores, but the properly attuned reader (such as yourself) will be able to divine the secrets of the universe from its very pages!

Well, maybe not. But it's a pretty darn good book all the same.

Here's a summary of what you'll find:

Chapter 1, "Blast Off," is a collection of tips for launching, managing, and closing Windows applications. You'll find out how to use the Windows Program Manager and File Manager, how to give Windows a new face, how to launch multiple applications, and how to exit applications quickly.

Chapter 2, "Doing DOS," covers all those applications that aren't written specifically for Windows. You'll learn how to write and edit PIF files, how to optimize the memory requirements for non-Windows applications, and what *not* to do with Windows.

Chapter 4, "Prints Charming," discusses downloading fonts, printing to disk, dealing with PostScript, and increasing printing speed and efficiency.

Chapter 4, "Optimizing Your System," gets into some of the technical details that make Windows really interesting. This chapter reveals ways to tweak your memory, disk space, and system resources for maximum efficiency. Although excavating in the system files has traditionally been recommended only for the brave, you'll soon discover that you can make Windows roll over and purr.

Chapter 5, "Custom Made Windows," expands on the previous chapter. Once you have Windows running

## INTRODUCTION

smoothly in its "vanilla" format, you can start changing it to suit your personal working style. For example, how'd you like to put your own custom start-up screen into Windows? Or maybe set your own custom screen colors? Design your own icons? It's all in this chapter.

Finally, Chapter 6, "Fun and Functional," gives you a taste of what's out there in the world to make your Windows computing life easier and more fun. Macros, sound, games, and screen savers are among the many subjects examined here. Most importantly, you'll learn how to cheat at Solitaire and Minesweeper.

The best way to use this book is by skimming it at first. Each of the tips has a summary in gray identification. When you find something you want to know more about, do a little serious reading. But, hey, if you just want to look up an occasional tip in the index, we won't mind a bit. That's a good way to use this book, too. We've arranged this book so you should be able to find something fascinating on almost every page. Check it out.

The information and hidden lore revealed to you in this book have cost us lifetimes. However, this copy of *101 Windows Tips & Tricks* only costs you the price of a paperback book.

Pretty cheap for the secrets of the universe.

**Launching, managing, and closing Windows applications**

**W**indows is an operating environment — a place to work (or play). It works with computer programs or *applications* (*apps* for short), be they giant spreadsheet programs or tiny memory-resident utilities. Because Windows lets you work and play the way you normally do — juggling several things at once — it behooves you to know how to get those balls in the air and bring them back down safely. Hence this chapter.

We'll start off with a quick overview of Program Manager and File Manager, Windows' built-in program launcher and file handler. Then we'll explore some other ways to start programs and automate your daily set-up process to save you time and trouble. After that, we'll throw in some tips on launching your data files. We'll close with the end of the process, namely turning your applications (and Windows) off.

CHAPTER 1

# Getting with the Program and File Managers

When you first install and start Windows, you see Program Manager, the centerpiece of the Windows interface. ProgMan (as we call it) can be fun and colorful, but it can also be a drag on your system's power. Nevertheless, it's flexible, free, and easy to use. In this section, we'll let you in on our favorite tricks for setting up and maintaining Program Manager and File Manager. We'll also show you a way to replace ProgMan with something better.

 ## Basic ProgMan skills

You probably already know how Program Manager works. But the following table will serve as a quick refresher. And you might discover something new.

**Program Manager Maneuvers**

| To accomplish this | Take this action |
| --- | --- |
| Launch an app | Double-click the icon |
| Launch an app minimized | Shift-double-click the icon |
| Move an icon to a different group | Drag the icon with the mouse |
| Copy an icon | Hold the Ctrl key and drag the icon |
| Delete an icon | Press Del and click Yes in the confirmation box (or press Y) |
| Arrange icons in group window | Drag them manually or choose Arrange Icons from the Window menu |
| Keep icons automatically arranged in group windows | Activate Auto Arrange on the Options menu |
| Keep icons the way you last left them | Arrange icons, deactivate Auto Arrange on the Options menu, exit Windows with Save Changes |
| Automatically minimize ProgMan each time you launch an app | Activate Minimize on Use on the Options menu |

4

# BLAST OFF

 ## Save time installing Windows apps

> To add multiple Windows applications to Program Manager in one swoop, arrange Program Manager and File Manager in side-by-side windows. Then drag the executable file from a File Manager directory window to a group in Program Manager.

The fastest way to add a whole bunch of Windows apps to ProgMan is to set up your desktop so the only two open windows are Program Manager and File Manager (FileMan for short). Double-click the desktop or press Ctrl-Esc to bring up Task Manager. Click the Tile button to make FileMan and ProgMan appear side by side (Figure 1-1). In File Manager, open the directory window(s) where your apps are located. In Program Manager, minimize all groups and choose Arrange Icons from the Windows menu. Select program filename(s) in FileMan and drag it (or them) to the group icon of your choice in ProgMan. (You can also drag them to open group windows, but keeping them all minimized ensures you can see all your groups at once.)

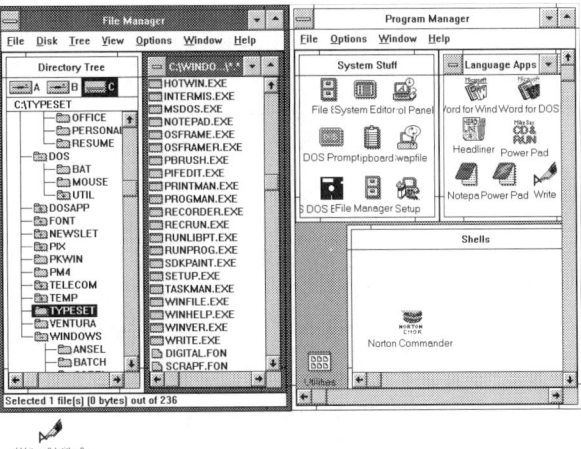

**Figure 1-1**
Tile File Manager and Program Manager, then drag a program file to the group of your choice.

Naturally, you may have to do some rearranging of icons and windows in ProgMan later. But it sure beats typing all those pathnames into ProgMan's Properties dialog box.

**Essential File Manager keyboard moves**

Many basic File Manager operations are possible without ever using a mouse. The table below summarizes some of the most important keyboard shortcuts.

Some people (like Scott) just don't like the slowdown of taking hands off the keyboard to grab the mouse. These keyboard shortcuts will help you zoom around File Manager without having to mouse around. For more shortcuts, see the tip "Speed climbing the directory tree," on page 8.

**Keyboard shortcuts for File Manager**

| To accomplish this | Press these keys |
|---|---|
| Switch among drive icons, tree, and contents list in same window | Tab or F6 |
| Switch among directory windows or icons | Ctrl-Tab or Ctrl-F6 |
| Log onto drive A, drive B, etc. | With a directory window highlighted and the selection bar in either the tree or directory pane, press Ctrl-A, Ctrl-B, etc. |
| Open a new directory window | Tab to the drive icons, cursor to the one you want, and press Enter |
| View properties of selected file | Alt-Enter |
| Tile directory windows in horizontal rows | Shift-F4 |
| Expand one level of a selected branch | + |
| Collapse one level of a selected branch | - (minus or hyphen) |

# BLAST OFF

| To accomplish this | Press these keys |
|---|---|
| Expand all levels below a selected branch | * |
| Expand all branches in the entire tree | Ctrl-* |
| Select all files in a contents window | Ctrl-/ |
| Select sequential files in a contents list | Cursor to first filename then hold Shift as you cursor up or down to select others |
| Select a group of non-sequential files in a contents list | Shift-F8, then cursor to each file you want and press the spacebar |
| Close a directory window | Ctrl-F4 |

## Speed climbing the directory tree

You can quickly navigate File Manager's directory tree without a mouse. The table below summarizes some of the most important keyboard shortcuts.

If you already have mouse in hand, clicking around the directory tree (to display a contents list) or double-clicking (to expand or collapse a branch) is the best way to go. But for keyboard freaks, here are some quick moves for getting around your directories and files without taking your hands off your keys.

### Tree-climbing in File Manager

| To move to this location | Press these keys |
|---|---|
| Directory above or below the current selection | Up or down arrow |
| Next highest branch while in tree | Left arrow or backspace |
| Next highest branch while in contents list | Home then Enter |
| First subdirectory under current directory (if visible) | Down or right arrow |
| Up one directory at same level | Ctrl-up arrow |
| Down one directory at same level | Ctrl-down arrow |
| Up one screenful | Page Up |
| Down one screenful | Page Down |
| Top of current tree or contents list | Home |

| To move to this location | Press these keys |
|---|---|
| Bottom of current tree or contents list | End |
| Next directory in tree beginning with *X*, etc. | *X*, etc. |
| Next filename in contents list beginning with *X*, etc. | *X*, etc. |

## Magic mouse moves in File Manager

You can also use a mouse to navigate File Manager's directory tree. The table below summarizes some of the most important mouse commands.

Drag-and-drop is the latest fad in graphical interfaces, and Windows 3.1 is not to be left out. You can accomplish all kinds of nifty things by dragging your File Manager files to various places. In addition, mouse moves vastly simplify a number of File Manager chores. The table below lists some of the most important.

### Major mouse moves in File Manager

| To accomplish this action | Make these moves |
| --- | --- |
| Log onto drive A, drive B, etc. | Click once on the drive A icon, drive B icon, etc. |
| Open a new directory window. | Double-click on the drive icon you want |
| Split (or change the split of) a directory window to show tree and contents list. | Choose Split from the View menu, position the split where you want, and click once. |
| Display the contents of a directory. | Click once on directory name in tree (contents list must be showing) |
| Expand or collapse a branch. | Double-click on directory name in tree |
| Select sequential files in a contents list. | Click the first filename in then hold Shift as you click the last filename |
| Select a group of non-sequential files in a contents list. | Shift-F8, Hold Ctrl as you click each file you want selected |
| Move selected file(s) to another directory. | Drag the selected file(s) to the branch you want on the tree |

# BLAST OFF

| To accomplish this action | Make these moves |
|---|---|
| Copy selected file(s) to another directory. | Hold Ctrl as you drag the selected file(s) to the branch you want on the tree |
| Copy selected file(s) to another drive. | Drag the selected file(s) to the drive icon you want |
| Print selected file(s) | With Print Manager running, drag the selected file(s) to the Print Manager window or icon |
| Add a file as an icon in Program Manager | Drag a selected file to a group in Program Manager |
| Embed an icon view of a file into the file of an OLE app | Drag the selected file into the OLE app's window |
| Link a file into the file of an OLE app | Holding Ctrl and Shift, drag the selected file into the OLE app's window |

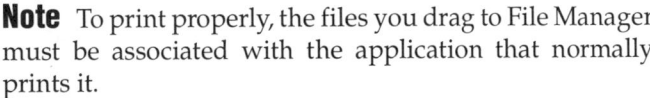 **Note** To print properly, the files you drag to File Manager must be associated with the application that normally prints it.

## CHAPTER 1

 **Giving Windows a new face**

> If you don't like Program Manager, you can replace it with another program, such as File Manager. Just edit SYSTEM.INI with a text editor. Find the line that says *shell=progman.exe*. In place of *progman.exe*, insert your program's filename. Save the file and restart Windows.

If you just don't like Program Manager, you can replace it with a different program launcher — or just about any program. For example, if you often launch your programs from File Manager (perhaps with techniques you'll learn later in this chapter), you can make File Manager your *shell* — the program that always starts with Windows and exits Windows when you close it.

To change your shell, find the SYSTEM.INI file in your Windows directory. Save a backup copy of the file, then open it with Notepad or another text editor. Find the line that reads:

    shell=progman.exe

Replace *progman.exe* with the executable filename of your choice. For example, to make File Manager your shell, your shell= line should read:

    shell=winfile.exe

Now save the file and exit Windows. The next time you start Windows, your new shell will appear in place of Program Manager.

**Note** Only certain programs can act as Windows' shell. Check with the manufacturer before investing in a shell replacement.

For more ideas on replacing your Windows shell, see Chapter 5, "Custom Made Windows."

12

# Lifting Off

Your average work or play session begins with launching and setting up the programs you need. This can involve several steps every time you begin a Windows session. But with the tricks you'll learn here, we'll show you how to combine and automate steps to relieve you of unnecessary and repetitive chores. You'll learn how to:

- Automatically launch applications when you start windows
- Automatically size and position windows
- Launch multiple applications simultaneously
- Assign keyboard shortcuts for quick launches

# CHAPTER 1

 **Easy autostarting of multiple apps**

> To automatically launch applications when you start Windows, drag a copy of their icons to the Startup Group.

You can automatically launch your favorite apps every time you start Windows. And it's simpler than ever with Windows 3.1.

Program Manager includes a group called StartUp. Any applications you put in the group will start automatically each time you start Windows.

To place an application in the StartUp group, just drag its icon to the StartUp icon or into its open group windows. If you want to keep copies of these applications in their original groups, hold down the Ctrl key as you drag the icon.

If you want any of these applications to start minimized, select the icon and press Alt-Enter to open its Properties dialog box. Then check the Run Minimized box and click OK (Figure 1-2).

**Figure 1-2**
To autostart applications when you start Windows, move or copy their icons into the StartUp group.

## Alternate autostarting of multiple apps

> Another way to launch applications when you start Windows is to edit WIN.INI. Adding executable filenames to the run= line starts the app in a window. Adding executable filenames to the load= line starts the app as an icon.

Even if Program Manager is not your shell of choice (see "Giving Windows a new face" earlier in this chapter) or if you are still using Windows 3.0, you can still automatically launch your favorite apps every time you start Windows. All it takes is a little editing of the WIN.INI file in your Windows directory. You'll learn more about WIN.INI in Chapter 5, "Custom Made Windows." For now, we're only interested in using it to launch apps.

The first thing to do whenever editing WIN.INI (or any INI file) is to save a backup copy — just in case you screw things up. After that, you can open WIN.INI in an ASCII editor like Notepad (or a word processor as long as you save it in a text-only format).

Now find the run= and load= lines at the beginning of the WIN.INI file. To autostart a program in an open window, type its executable filename after run=. To autostart a program as an icon on your desktop, use the load= line. If your app is not in a directory listed in your DOS PATH command (in your AUTOEXEC.BAT file), you should include the full path with the filename. To start multiple programs, separate the names with either a single space or a comma — but not both. The limit per line is 127 characters.

For example, if you wanted to autostart Excel and Windows Clock utility in open windows and place the Word for Windows icon on your desktop, your run= and load= lines would look like this:

```
load=c:\winword\winword.exe
run=c:\excel\excel.exe clock.exe
```

This gimmick also works for DOS programs. Just type in either the executable filename and path, or the name of the program's PIF file. Note, however, that if two or more full-screen DOS applications are listed on the run= line, only the last one listed will open full screen.

 **Note** Not all programs that can act as Windows' shell will support this use of WIN.INI's run= and load= lines. (Fortunately, File Manager does.) Check with your application's manufacturer to be certain.

BLAST OFF

 **Custom autostarting one application**

> To control which application launches each time you start Windows, type WIN at the DOS prompt, followed by the application's executable filename. You can also add the name of a data file after the program's executable filename.

If you want the same application(s) to run each time you start Windows, consult the previous tip. But perhaps more than one person uses a computer, or perhaps you simply want to start your Windows session with a different app on different occasions. No problem.

The secret to starting a different application with each Windows session is the command you use to startup Windows from the DOS prompt. Just type WIN as you usually do, but then add a space and the name of your program's executable file. If your application is not on your DOS path (as specified in your AUTOEXEC.BAT), you should also add the path information. For example, to start Windows and PageMaker simultaneously, you would type the following line at the DOS prompt:

    WIN PM4.EXE

Simple, no? The disadvantage is you can only start one application this way (plus any you have in Program Manager's StartUp group).

You can also load a particular data file from the DOS prompt. Just add the name of the data file after the program's executable filename. For example, to open a PageMaker newsletter file called NEWS.PM4 at the same time you start Windows, enter the following line at the DOS prompt:

    WIN PM4.EXE NEWS.PM4

 **Hint** If your data file is *associated* with your application, you can leave off the executable file name and just type WIN followed by the data filename. For more on associating data files with programs, turn to "When Your Heart Belongs to Data" later in this chapter.

17

# CHAPTER 1

 **Custom autostarting of multiple apps**

Utilities such as Run (from Dragon's Eye Software) and Power Launcher (from hDC) let you launch multiple apps from the command line.

The last tip explained how to autostart a different program each time you start Windows. But that only works for one program. What if you want a whole different *set* of applications on your desktop each time you climb into Windows? You can with utilities like Run and Power Launcher.

Run comes as part of the Dragon's Eye Utilities ($10 shareware). Just type WIN at the DOS prompt, followed by the RUN command and your executable filenames separated by a comma *and* a space. (You have the DOS-imposed limit of 127 characters.) You can also add command-line parameters, including the name of any data file you want loaded. For example, the command line below starts Windows and uses Run to launch Windows Clock and a file (called README.WRI) in Windows Write:

```
win run clock, write c:\doc\readme.wri
```

Here are some hot tips on different ways to use Run:

- Using a text editor, type a command (like the above example) that starts Windows with a useful collection of programs. Then save the file with a .BAT extension. To start this set of programs with Windows, just type the batch filename at the DOS prompt. Repeat for as many custom configurations as you want, or for as many users that use the computer.

- Create an icon in Program Manager. On the command line (Properties dialog box), type a run command that includes the programs you want (there's an 80-character limit). The next time you double-click this icon, it will start all the apps you listed.

- Use Run's WIN.INI option as explained in the Run documentation. You can then start the programs you listed in WIN.INI by simply typing WIN RUN at the DOS prompt. The advantage over using WIN.INI's run= and load= lines is that Run lets you add any command-line parameters your program may need.

 hDC's Power Launcher works in a similar fashion but adds new commands so you can control not only what launches, but how (as full screen, as a window, as an icon, and so on).

## ➤ Easy positioning of windows

*The utility RunProg lets you set the startup size and position (and directory) of Windows apps.*

Some Windows applications (including Windows Help) remember the last size and position of their window, and open that way the next time you start them. Unfortunately, many apps are not so accommodating. One solution is to create a Recorder macro that launches and resizes windows the way you want. But Recorder can be frustrating — one mistake and you have to start all over. For a one-shot solution, you need a separate utility.

For example, with BatchWorks from Publishing Technologies, you can create a macro that launches your application and then resizes it to your specs (use the RUN and WINPLACE commands). The pop-up menu program Launch also lets you designate window size and position, simplified with an "easy sizing" button. Or you can specify screen position with hDC's Power Launcher.

But if you only want to set the startup directory and change the window size, your least expensive option ($10 plus disk fee) is David Feinleib's RunProg. RunProg requires some fiddling with the command line of your icon's Properties dialog box. You launch RunProg and let it launch the app so it comes up the way you want it. You specify whether to launch the program maximized (full screen), minimized (as an icon), normal (its default size), hidden (so it's invisible), or by specifying exact screen coordinates of the window's size and position. The example in Figure 1-3 starts Notepad running full screen with a startup directory of C:\DOC.

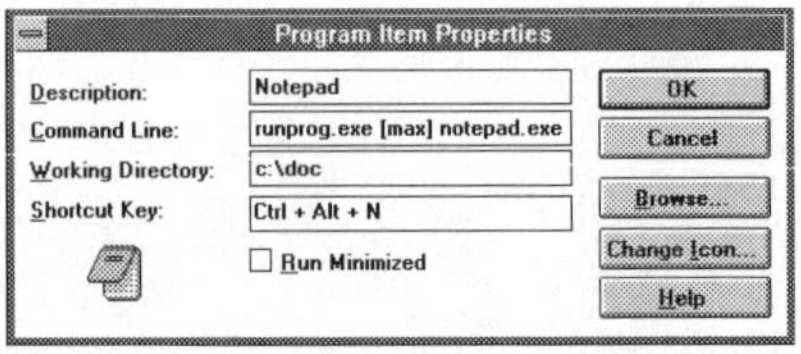

**Figure 1-3**
RunProg lets you specify not only a startup directory, but also the size and position of your apps window.

For more powerful ways to customize application startup, see "Fast launching of multiple applications," on page 22.

**BLAST OFF**

 **Quick trick for resizing a window**

To quickly make your application fill your screen except for the lower area containing icons, minimize all apps but the one to be resized, start Task Manager (Ctrl-Esc), and press Alt-T.

Our favorite window arrangement is one in which the window fills the screen except for a strip along the bottom so you can see what icons are on your desktop. Fortunately, there is a relatively quick way to obtain this position without using utilities or macros. Here's how:

1. Make sure the application you want to resize is the only open window on the desktop. If you haven't launched the app yet, minimize your other apps, then launch the app to be resized. (You must have at least one other app open besides the one to be resized.)

2. Double-click the desktop or press Ctrl-Esc to bring up Task Manager (Figure 1-4).

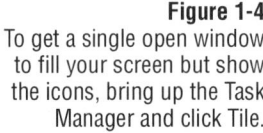

**Figure 1-4**
To get a single open window to fill your screen but show the icons, bring up the Task Manager and click Tile.

3. Click Tile or press Alt-T.

Ta-da! When Windows tiles a single app, it spreads it out to cover the whole desktop except the bottom. With many apps, you can press the keys while the app is still loading, then sit back and wait for it to load and resize itself.

21

# CHAPTER 1

 **Fast launching of multiple applications**

> *PC Magazine's* WinSaver restores the arrangement of your application windows as they were when you exited Windows. hDC's WorkSets (part of the $99 FirstApps) lets you create custom arrangements of application windows and launch them with one command.

Launching applications to custom-sized windows is one thing. But what if you regularly work with different groups of programs for different tasks? Or what if several people use the same computer, but want to autostart a different application than the last person? Or what if you just want Windows to start with your apps arranged the way you left them? One solution is Run from Dragon's Eye Software (discussed earlier in this chapter). Here are two other, more powerful, utilities that fill the bill:

### WinSaver
WinSaver, free from *PC Magazine*, remembers the last applications you used so your next Windows session can start up where you left off. You can also have WinSaver prompt you to save the current arrangement before you exit. The only thing it can't remember is the *state* of your programs — what data files were loaded, arrangement of child windows, zoom level, and so on. But the price is right and it's much faster than setting up apps manually.

### Work Sets (hDC FirstApps)
FirstApps is a $99.95 collection of utilities from hDC Corporation. One of these is Work Sets, a utility that records your precise screen arrangement and lets you store it as a "Work Set," or application group. When you later launch a Work Set, all the apps in the group are loaded, complete with their original size and position. Work Sets can even remember what documents were loaded in your apps, though not other internal states such as arrangement of child windows. If you like, Work Sets will optionally save changes upon exiting, for continuity between Windows sessions. FirstApps' launching system is a memory resident utility that lets you start individual Work Sets from any application's system menu.

# BLAST OFF

 ## No-frills quick launching of many apps

> The fastest way to launch multiple applications without macros or utilities is to Shift-double click a series of icons in Program Manager.

If you don't want the cost and trouble of a utility, here's the fastest way to launch multiple applications:

With Program Manager open on your desktop, open the group windows containing the applications you want. Then hold down the Shift key and double-click on one icon after another until all your applications are launched (Figure 1-5).

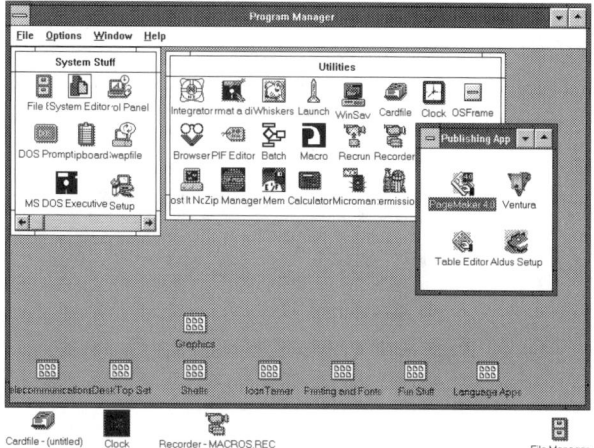

**Figure 1-5**
For quick launches of multiple apps, open the groups containing the apps you want, hold down the Shift key, and double-click one icon after another.

Holding the Shift key while you double-click does two things: it launches each application as an icon, and it overrides the "Minimize on Use" option if it's checked in Program Manager's Options menu. The effect is you can stay in Program Manager and keep double-clicking until you've got what you want.

The disadvantage is that all of your applications are now icons and you will have to double-click on them (this time on the desktop) to open their windows. Okay, it's not ideal, but what did you expect for no money? If this isn't good enough for you, check out the next tip.

# CHAPTER 1

 **Saving steps with app-starting macros**

> To launch and arrange one or more applications, try creating a Windows Recorder macro. Record a shortcut that switches to Program Manager (via the Alt-Tab shortcut) and uses the Run command (File menu) to launch your app(s).

Wouldn't it be great if you could launch your favorite apps with just a keystroke or two instead of mousing around? With Windows Recorder, you can . Here's how:

1. Start Recorder, open the macro file of your choice, and begin recording your macro. Set playback to "Same Application."

2. With the Alt key held down, press Tab until Program Manager (or its icon) is highlighted.

> **Note** If Program Manager is already highlighted, you *must* press Tab as many times as necessary to cycle through the other programs and then return to Program Manager.

3. Press Alt-F, R to open the Run dialog box. Type in the path and name of your program's executable file. For example, in creating a macro that launches Excel, type:

   `c:\excel\excel.exe`

   If you want it to start as an icon, press Alt-M. Then press Enter.

> **Hint** At this point, you can add optional steps to further customize your macros. For example, you can move or resize your program's window(s). You could also add a step that prompts you for a data file (Alt-F, O for most programs). Or, if you want the macro to launch multiple programs, just repeat steps 2 and 3 until you're satisfied.

4. When you're done, press Ctrl-Break, select Save Macro (or press Alt-S) and click OK.

The only problem with Recorder is you have to do things right the first time — if you make a mistake you must start the recording all over. For more information on creating Recorder macros, see your *Microsoft Windows User's Guide*.

## Superior hotkey launching

> If you don't use Program Manager as your shell, you can still launch applications with keyboard shortcuts by purchasing Launch or HotKey, both under $100.

In Windows 3.1, Program Manager lets you assign Shortcut keys that, when pressed, launch an application or switch to it if it's already running. Unfortunately, ProgMan requires that all shortcuts include the clumsy Ctrl-Alt or Ctrl-Alt-Shift combination. In addition, if you use File Manager (or some other app) as your shell, you won't be able to use these shortcut keys. (See "Giving Windows a new face" on page 12.)

Recorder (see previous tip) provides a dandy way to launch and arrange apps with a quick keystroke. But if you want a shortcut that switches you to a running app, you must create a new macro, and that means taking up another key assignment. Instead, try:

### HotKey

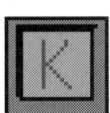
HotKey is a $20 shareware utility that lets you assign shortcut keys (hotkeys) for launching up to 32 programs. The first time you press your assigned hotkey sequence, your program is launched. If the program is already running, pressing the hotkey switches you to that window — handy if the app is minimized or buried under other windows. Unfortunately, this does not allow launching multiple copies (instances) of programs for those that allow it (like Notepad). The utility also includes shortcuts for minimizing and maximizing the active window.

### Launch

Launch features a configurable pop-up menu for starting applications. It's twice as expensive as HotKey, but has lots more features and the best hotkey support. Like HotKey, Launch's shortcuts start applications. In addition, if your application is already running, your hotkey will either launch a new copy of the program (if it supports multiple instances) or merely switch you to the program's window. Launch can even replace Program Manager as your Windows shell.

# When Your Heart Belongs to Data

So far we've been taking an approach that's pretty standard in the DOS world — first launching your program, then loading in the data file you need to work on. But Windows also lets you save time by combining these tasks into one step. The secret is *associating* your data file's three-letter extension with the application you need to modify it.

You probably already know how: launch File Manager and open a directory window. Select a filename that has the extension you want to associate with an application. Then choose the Associate command from the File menu. Either select your application from the list box or (if it's not there), type the complete path and name of the application's executable file. If the program is on your DOS search PATH (as specified in your AUTOEXEC.BAT file), you can omit path information. Finally, click OK. For example, Figure 1-6 shows the link between PageMaker 4 files and its executable file.

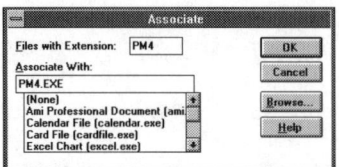

**Figure 1-6**
File Manager's Associate dialog box.

Many applications create this association when you install them, but others require you do it yourself. This section will tell you how to get the most out this Windows feature.

BLAST OFF

 **Quick launching of data files**

> You can launch an associated data file by double-clicking the filename in a file utility or entering the name in an icon's Properties dialog. You can autostart a data file by moving its icon to Windows' Startup group or adding the name to WIN.INI's load= or run= line.

Once your data files are associated with your application, you can launch the application with the file in one quick step. Here are some possibilities:

- Double-click the filename of your choice in File Manager or almost any Windows file utility (Figure 1-7).

**Figure 1-7**
Launch an associated file by double-clicking its filename.

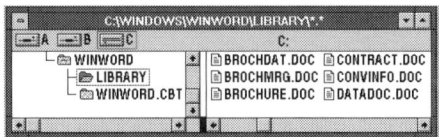

- Enter the path and name of your data file on the command line of a Program Manager icon. Select the icon and choose Properties from the File menu (Figure 1-8).

 **Hint** You can find many excellent icons for your documents by clicking Change Icon in the Program Item Properties dialog box and typing PROGMAN.EXE in the File Name text box. Click OK, then click Change Icon again.

**Figure 1-8**
Type an associated filename in an icon's Properties box.

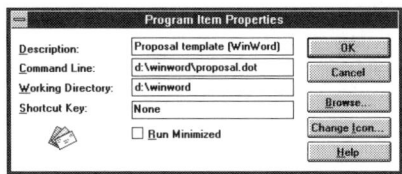

- After turning the data file into an icon (see above), copy or move the icon to Program Manager's StartUp group to automatically launch the file when you start Windows (Figure 1-9).

27

## CHAPTER 1

**Figure 1-9**
Use WIN.INI to autostart applications with an associated data file.

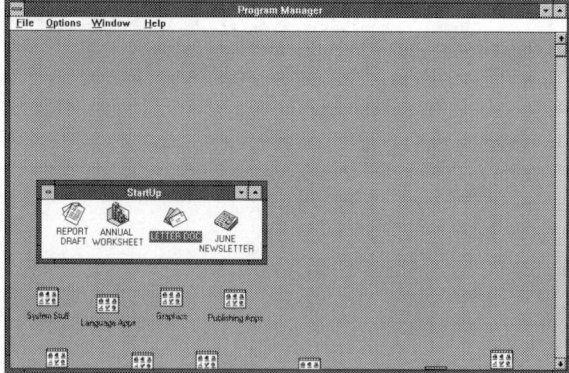

## ▶ Handy text file associations

> Associating your favorite ASCII editor with the file extensions listed here can speed up routine file reading and editing.

When you installed Windows, it automatically associated its ASCII editor Notepad with files having the .TXT extension. But text files come with all kinds of extensions. Consider associating the following extensions with NOTEPAD.EXE (or your favorite ASCII editor). That way, when you're digging through directories with your file utility, you can quickly open these files.

### Common ASCII extensions

| Extension | Common use |
|---|---|
| 1ST | Common extension for README.1ST files (such as those that come with new software) |
| ASC | Common extension for ASCII files |
| ASP | Extension for scripts created with Procomm Plus |
| BAK | Common extension for backup files, such as old versions of AUTOEXEC.BAT |
| BAT | Common extension for DOS batch files (see note below) |
| CFG | Common extension for configuration files |
| CHP | Ventura Publisher chapter files |
| GEN | Ventura Publisher generated files |
| INI | Initialization files that give Windows or your applications information they need when they start up |
| ME | Common extension for READ.ME files (such as those that come with new software) |

CHAPTER 1

| Extension | Common use |
|---|---|
| OK | Common extension for README.OK files (such as those that come with new software) |
| OLD | Common extension for backup files, such as old versions of AUTOEXEC.BAT |
| SYD | Backup files created by Windows' System Configuration Editor (SYSEDIT.EXE) |
| SYS | Common extension for configuration files such as CONFIG.SYS |
| TOO | Common extension for README.TOO files (such as those that come with new software) |

***Warning*** You shouldn't (and can't) associate BAT files with a text editor until you've taken the steps explained in this chapter under the next tip, "Easy editing of batch files."

## ➤ Easy editing of batch files

> If you prefer to run batch files with PIFs, you can simplify batch file editing in Windows. First, remove bat from WIN.INI's Programs= line. Then associate BAT files with a text editor.

Wouldn't it be handy to have your DOS batch files associated with a text editor for quick opening and editing? You can, but not without some special preparation. Windows treats batch files like program files — if you double-click a batch filename in File Manager, Windows will execute the commands specified in the batch. So you have to take three steps to set it up right:

Open WIN.INI with Notepad or another ASCII editor. In the first section, under the heading [windows], look for a line that reads

```
Programs=com exe bat pif
```

This is the line that tells Windows to execute BAT files (Figure 1-10). Simply delete the "bat" from this line. Then save the WIN.INI file, and restart Windows.

**Figure 1-10**
To associate BAT files with an ASCII editor, first find the "programs=" line in WIN.INI.

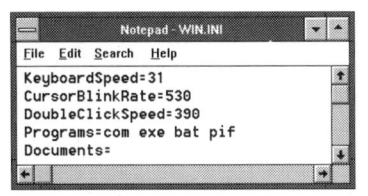

```
                    Notepad - WIN.INI
File  Edit  Search  Help
KeyboardSpeed=31
CursorBlinkRate=530
DoubleClickSpeed=390
Programs=com exe bat pif
Documents=
```

Second, associate BAT files with your favorite text editor as explained on page 25. The next time you double-click a batch filename, you'll be able to edit it, not watch it run.

Finally, make a PIF (program information file) for each batch file you want to execute from inside Windows. To execute the batch, you will launch the PIF, not the BAT file.

For more about PIF files, see Chapter 2, "Doing DOS."

# Making a Soft Landing

Just as important as knowing how to get your applications up and running is the ability to make a graceful exit. Otherwise, you may lose the data you've been working on. We'll show you our favorite ways to get out of Windows, such as:

- Exiting quickly with the mouse or the keyboard
- Using Closer from Dragon's Eye Software to exit apps
- Closing applications with WinExit, a public domain program

# BLAST OFF

## ▶ Quick escapes

> There are several speedy shortcuts for closing applications. The best mouse method is to double-click the Control-menu box. The best keyboard method is to press Alt-F4.

You probably already know the standard ways to quit programs, but here's a quick review:

- To close an open window fast, double-click on its Control-menu box.

- Choose Close from your program's Control menu (this works with both open Windows and icons)

- Choose Exit (or Quit) from your program's File menu.

- When the proper application window or icon is active, press Alt-F4.

- Double-click the desktop (or press Ctrl-Esc) to open Task Manager. Select the name of the application you wish to close and click the End Task button (or press Alt-E).

- Exiting Windows will close all applications automatically — unless they're DOS applications. If you are running in 386 Enhanced mode, you can allow Windows to close these as well. Just open the application's PIF (using PIF Editor), click the Advanced button, and check the box labelled Allow Close When Active. (Only use this option for applications that don't write to disk; *never* use with word processors, spreadsheets, or databases.)

## ▶ Closing the invisible

> If you need to close many programs quickly or close a program whose icon is hidden, use Closer, part of a $10 utility set from Dragon's Eye Software. Closer lets you shut down hidden apps from a handy dialog box.

A growing number of Windows utilities operate the way TSR (terminate and stay resident) programs do in DOS: they hang around in memory until they are needed; even the icon is (or may be) hidden. Screen savers are a good example of this kind of Windows program.

But here's the problem: if you can't see a program's window or icon, how do you shut it down? The process, if one exists, can be time consuming.

A faster method is to get Closer, which comes in the $10 Dragon's Eye Utilities, the same collection that includes Run (discussed earlier). Double-click the Closer icon and you have a dialog box listing all the applications running under Windows — even the hidden ones (Figure 1-11). Just select the one you want to close and click the Close button. Repeat until you're satisfied. Then use Closer to close itself.

**Figure 1-11**
Closer lets you shut down even hidden applications.

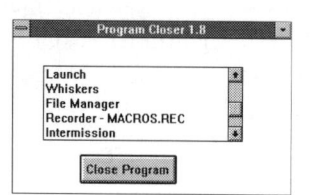

If you use Program Manager, launching Closer only to close one application is hardly worth the effort. But if you need to close several applications, or if you have easy access to Closer through a quick-launching utility like Launch, then Closer becomes a real convenience.

# BLAST OFF

## ▶ Saving time with WinExit

> WinExit is a freebie (public domain) utility that gives you multiple options for quickly exiting Windows.

Shutting down Windows means exiting from the Windows *shell* program — the default program that starts when Windows does, usually Program Manager. If you keep Program Manager minimized, you can exit by selecting the icon, then choosing Close. If you keep Program Manager open, a quick double-click of the system menu ends things. Either way, you have to confirm your decision. If you tire of this two-step process or simply want more options, you need a Windows exiting utility.

There are a number of such utilities available, but the most flexible is WinExit, which is available as public domain software on many electronic bulletin boards. WinExit lets you customize the way you get out of Windows. Here are some possibilities:

- *Exit by double-clicking the WinExit icon on the desktop.* Load WinExit automatically each time using the ProgMan's StartUp group (as explained earlier).

- *Exit by double-clicking the WinExit icon in Program Manager.* Just enter the proper command-line parameters to the icon's properties.

- *Exit by using a menu-based program launcher.* Even if you don't use Program Manager as your shell, WinExit's command-line options let you exit from menu-based utilities such hDC's Windows Express or the Metz Task Manager.

No matter which of the above *locations* you exit from, WinExit lets you customize the *method* of exiting. You can:

- Exit with the usual Program Manager warning box that lets you save changes to Program Manager groups and icon arrangements.

- Exit with a simple warning box (without reference to Program Manager).

- Exit with no warning at all — double-click and poof!

35

CHAPTER 1

# Summing Up

This has been a chapter of starts and stops. You learned the fastest ways to get into your applications and the safest ways to get out.

In the next chapter, we'll deal with the vagaries of a specific class of applications, namely those not designed specifically for Windows. Surprisingly, Windows gives your DOS apps even more power and punch than your Windows applications. But how will you tap that power? Keep reading.

# Doing DOS

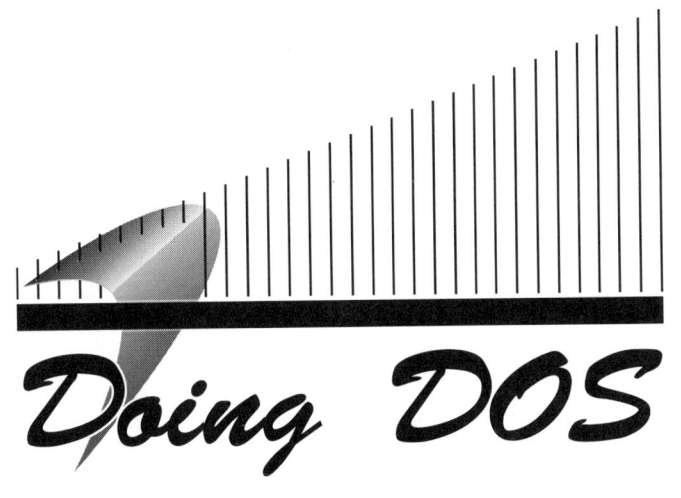

**Achieving maximum cooperation from non-Windows applications**

Let's face it: although Windows was an instant success with millions of users, its debut by no means spells the end of character-based applications. Indeed, much of the reason users embrace Windows is its marvelous ability to support and even enhance non-Windows applications. In fact, users of 386 enhanced mode actually have more multitasking power and control over non-Windows applications than they do over Windows apps.

It's only appropriate, then, that we devote some attention to our favorite tweaks and tricks for getting DOS applications to run their best under Windows. This chapter will teach you how to:

- Use the PIF editor to get optimal performance from your DOS applications
- Maximize memory for your non-Windows apps
- Exploit the hidden powers of your PIF's Optional Parameters box
- Avoid problematic pitfalls

## CHAPTER 2

> **Hint** A number of tips in other chapters relate equally to Windows and non-Windows applications. To get the full scoop on DOS-related tips, skim the rest of this book for items not covered in this chapter. For a fast glance, use the summary blocks at the top of each page.

# PIF the Magic DOS Gun

Windows runs DOS applications according to the settings in a *program information file*, or PIF for short. PIFs tell Windows how much memory the application needs, what video mode to use (text or graphics), what directory to start the program in, which command-line switches or parameters to give the program, whether to let the application override Windows' shortcut keys, and other information. If you are running in 386 enhanced mode, the PIF also specifies other options, including controls for multitasking and running in a window.

Each time you launch a program with the extension EXE, COM, or BAT, Windows looks in its own directory or the directory of the program for a PIF file matching the name of the executable file (WP.PIF for WP.EXE, COMMAND.PIF for COMMAND.COM, and so on). If it can't find a PIF, it relies on generic settings presumed to work with most applications.

Translated, that means you can run your DOS applications without ever peeking in a PIF — or for that matter even understanding what one is. But the default settings of Windows PIF files are intended to work for as many programs as possible. By adjusting the settings to your particular programs and needs, you can enhance the way your DOS apps run and acquire some time-saving shortcuts. Although most of this chapter deals with PIF settings, this section will start you out with some PIF settings that will shift your DOS apps into high gear:

- Adjusting PIFs for instant speed up
- Switching options on the fly
- Turning off hotkeys
- Executing DOS commands via icons

CHAPTER 2

## ▶ PIF settings for instant speed up

> When you don't need other apps running in the background, checking the PIF Editor's Exclusive option (Execution section, 386 enhanced mode) will let your DOS application run faster.

If you (1) run Windows in 386 enhanced mode and (2) don't need other applications working in the background, this simple trick can increase the running speed of your DOS applications. Here's how:

1. Launch Windows' PIF Editor and open the PIF file for a DOS application.

▶ **Note** If you don't have a PIF file that corresponds to your DOS application, you can create one using the PIF Editor. See your *Microsoft Windows User's Guide* for details.

2. In the Execution section, check the box marked Exclusive (Figure 2-1).

**Figure 2-1**
You can speed up DOS programs in 386 enhanced mode by checking the Exclusive option.

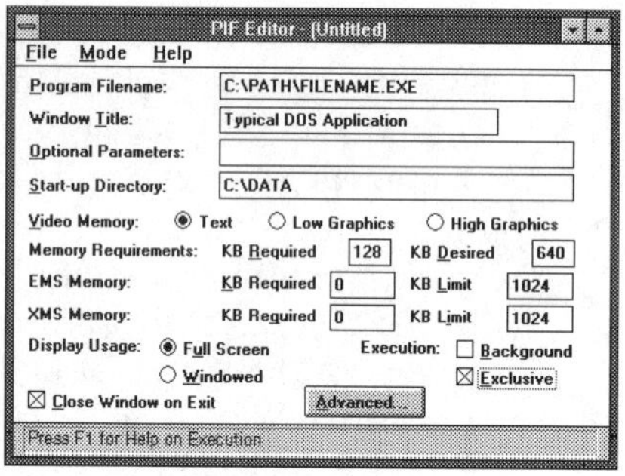

3. Save the PIF file.

Checking the Exclusive option means that whenever your DOS app is active, no other applications can work in the background. But it also means that Windows can devote more of its resources to your application. This trick will speed you up even if you don't have any other applications running at the same time as your DOS application.

If you want to be able to change this setting on the fly, see the next tip.

## ▶ Changing multitasking options

> To change the multitasking options for a non-Windows application while it is running in enhanced mode, press Alt-Spacebar to open the system menu, then press T to open the Settings dialog. Select the options you want and click OK.

The last tip told you how to speed up your DOS applications in 386 enhanced mode by turning off multitasking with the Exclusive option. The disadvantage is you won't be able to run other programs in the background. Fortunately, you can easily change this setting for individual sessions as you work.

While in your DOS app, hold down the Alt key while you press the spacebar. This opens the system menu for your current application. Then press T (or choose Settings with your mouse). The resulting dialog box lets you change multitasking options, switch between windowed or full-screen display, or terminate (Figure 2-2). To toggle the Exclusive option, press X (or select the check box with the mouse). Then click OK or press Enter.

**Figure 2-2**
This easily accessed dialog box lets you change settings for DOS apps while they are running.

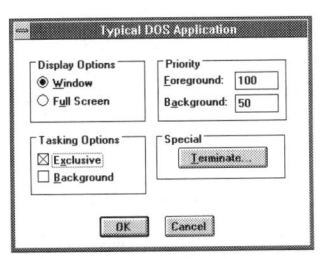

If your preferred work habits involve lots of multitasking, leave the Exclusive option unchecked in your PIF file (see previous tip). Then use this on-the-fly method when nothing else is operating. On the other hand, if you seldom run programs in the background, keep the Exclusive option checked as your normal setting and use this dialog box when you need programs running in the background.

▶ **Note** Checking the Exclusive option doesn't prevent you from switching between multiple programs. It merely means that the background programs are frozen while you work in the active (foreground) program.

CHAPTER 2

## ▶ Erasing a hot key

> To erase a DOS application's shortcut key in the PIF Editor (386 enhanced mode), click in the Application Shortcut Key text box and press Ctrl-Shift-Backspace.

For users of 386 enhanced mode, Windows makes it easy to assign "shortcut keys" to your DOS applications. These keys won't launch a DOS application, but they will switch you directly back to a DOS application that's already running.

Setting the key is simple. Use the Advanced button to open the Advanced Options dialog box in Windows PIF Editor (Figure 2-3). Move to the Application Shortcut Key text box. Now press the key combination you want for your shortcut. Click OK and save your PIF file.

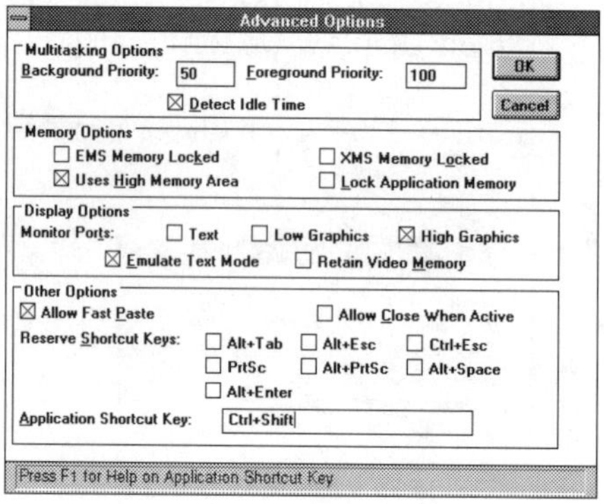

**Figure 2-3**
To erase an existing Application Shortcut Key, click in the text box and press Ctrl-Shift-Backspace.

The problem comes when you change your mind and want to use the shortcut for a macro or some other application. How do you erase the shortcut and replace it with nothing? Simple. Return to the Application Shortcut Key text box as before. Then press Ctrl-Shift-Backspace.

# DOING DOS

## ▶ Shortcuts for common DOS commands

> You can execute common DOS commands from icons. First create a PIF that launches COMMAND.COM. In the PIF's Optional Parameters box, type /c followed by the DOS command you want. Then create a Program Manager icon for the PIF.

Maybe you're so used to DOS that you just find it simpler to type common commands at the DOS prompt than to use File Manager or some other Windows utility. If so, you can save time by creating a PIF for each command you use most often.

Here's how: create a PIF that launches COMMAND.COM (in the Program Filename box). Then, in the Optional Parameters box, type /c followed by the command you want. Enter an appropriate description in the Window Title box and save the PIF. For example, Figure 2-4 shows a PIF that copies the contents of a directory to a floppy drive — handy for daily backups. Our picture shows an enhanced mode PIF, but any mode will do.

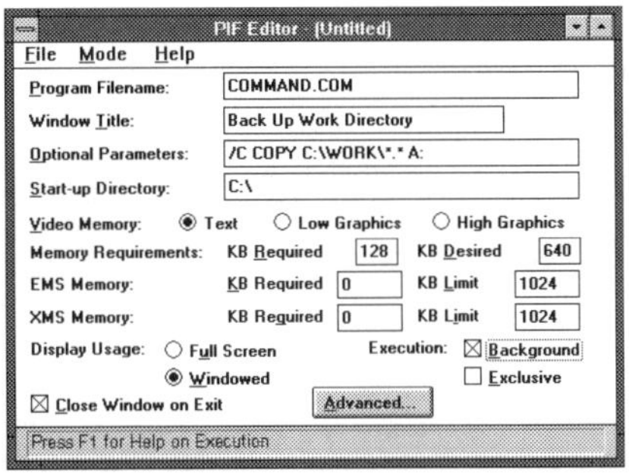

**Figure 2-4**
Using the /c parameter, you can create PIFs that launch common DOS commands.

The final step is to assign the PIF to an icon. Then, to execute the command, just double-click the icon, and away you go.

43

CHAPTER 2

# Parameter Power

Don't think we're through with PIFs yet. Although the last section taught you some clever tricks, you ain't seen nothing yet.

One of the most powerful features of PIF files is their ability to pass command-line parameters to your DOS applications. You just type the proper information in the PIF Editor's Optional Parameters text box. This may seem an obvious feature, but we'll show you ways to get extra power from those parameters. You'll learn how to:

- Use Optional Parameters for quick launches of data files

- Create multiple PIFs for custom start-ups of a single application

- Make Windows ask you for command-line parameters on the fly

## DOING DOS

### ▶ Quick launching of data files

> If your DOS application supports filenames on the command line, use File Manager to associate the data file's extension with your application's PIF. The Optional Parameters line must be blank.

Many DOS applications will open or manipulate a data file when the filename is listed on the command line that starts the program. For those apps, here's a time-saver: make sure your app's PIF has nothing in the Optional Parameters box (if it does, create a new PIF and leave Optional Parameters blank). Then use File Manager to associate your data file's extension with the PIF. Now each time you double-click a data file in File Manager (or other file utility), the data file will be loaded in your DOS application as soon as it opens.

Here's a useful example involving the popular utility PKZip, a shareware product from PKWARE, Inc. (PKZIP compresses files; PKUNZIP decompresses them.) To quickly decompress any file with the ZIP extension, create a PIF for PKUNZIP.EXE (Figure 2-5).

**Figure 2-5**
For quick unzipping, create a PIF that launches PKUNZIP.

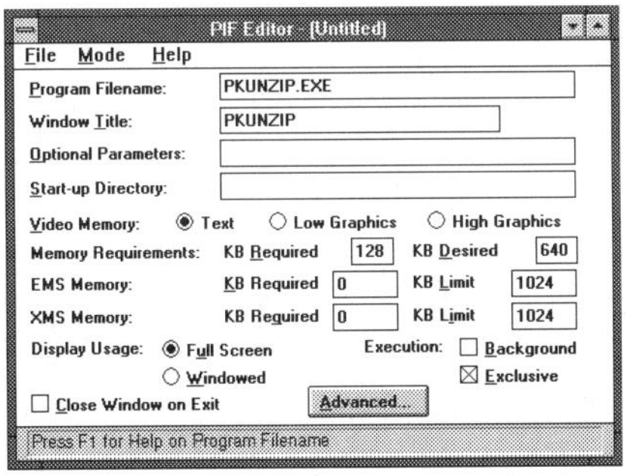

Next, launch Windows File Manager and select a filename with the extension ZIP. Choose Associate from the File menu and type in the name of your new PIF. Now when you double-click a ZIP filename, your PIF will automatically decompress the file(s) it contains.

45

## ▶ Easy customizing with multiple PIFs

> To create custom versions of the same DOS application, create multiple PIFs. Then launch your application from the PIF that suits your needs of the moment.

The trouble with PIF options is you don't always want your DOS application starting the same way. For example, sometimes you want your DOS word processor to start up in the WORK directory and other times you want it starting in the LETTER directory. Or maybe you want it launched with different command-line options.

The simplest solution is to create multiple PIFs, each having the parameters you want. Then launch your application from the PIF that has the options you want. If you use Program Manager as your launch point, just create a different icon for each PIF. If you use a menu-based program launcher (such as Launch or HotWin), you can create a different menu item for each PIF.

Here are some possibilities:

- Create PIFs that launch the same program but specify a different Start-up Directory in each. Then when you launch from that PIF, your program will open to the directory of your choice.

- Create PIFs that launch the same program but specify different Optional Parameters. For example, Microsoft Word 5.0 uses the /l (this is an "L," not a "one") parameter to open the program with the last document worked on. For other occasions, create a PIF that opens Word to a blank screen.

- If your app permits it, create PIFs that launch different scripts or macros. For example, Procomm Plus lets you create scripts that log onto electronic mail or bulletin board services. Try creating PIFs that launch different scripts with the Optional Parameters box. (For Procomm Plus, type /F followed by the script filename with no space in between.)

## ▶ Have Windows prompt you

> Another way to specify different parameters each time you start a DOS application is to type a question mark (?) in Optional Parameters text box. When you launch the application, Windows prompts you for the parameters you want.

In the last tip, you learned how to create different startup options for a single DOS app by creating different PIFs. That's the best way to go if you only start your app in a handful of different configurations. Much more than that, and you'll have to sort through too many icons to launch the configuration you want.

For the ultimate in flexibility, you can have Windows prompt you for the command-line parameters of your choice each time you start your DOS application. To use this feature, just type a question mark (?) in the Optional Parameters text box of Windows PIF Editor. The next time you start the application from this PIF, Windows displays a prompt like the one shown in Figure 2-6.

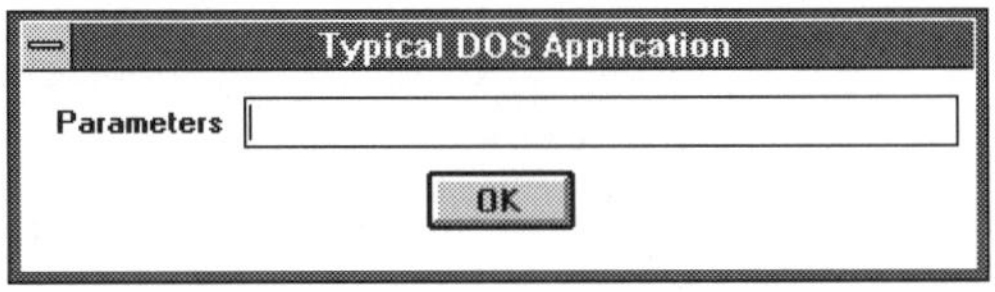

**Figure 2-6**
Adding a question mark to a PIF's Optional Parameters generates this prompt each time you launch the application.

All you do is type in a data filename or the command-line switches you want and press Enter (or click OK). What could be easier?

CHAPTER 2

# Down Memory Lane

Windows is a boon to those who had been struggling with the so-called 640K barrier that is the lot of all DOS users. It allowed users to access huge chunks of extended memory to run all kinds of applications, many of them simultaneously.

But Windows has not completely destroyed the 640K wall. DOS applications, not intended to run with other apps, will take as much memory as they can get. Windows has to parcel memory out to them by fooling those apps into thinking they're still running on a 640K machine. The upshot is you still have to be careful about what applications and utilities you load, when, and how.

This section will give you the advice you need to maximize the memory available to DOS applications running under Windows. You'll learn how to:

- Diagnose the amount of memory available to each DOS application
- Manage your mouse for an extra bit of memory
- Load your memory-resident utilities in the most efficient way
- Optimize memory use for 386 enhanced mode
- Use upper memory blocks

# DOING DOS

## ▶ Checking memory for DOS apps

> Each DOS application you run under Windows can only access some fraction of the first 640K available right before you start Windows. To discover this amount, type CHKDSK at the DOS prompt.

You might think that Windows' ability to manage tons of extended memory and run multiple non-Windows applications means that your DOS apps will never thirst for memory. You would, unfortunately, be wrong. The most RAM each DOS application will ever get from Windows is the amount of *conventional memory* (your machine's first 640K) you have available right before starting Windows, minus a little that Windows uses to work its magic.

That means the more memory-resident utilities you load before starting Windows (usually through your AUTOEXEC.BAT or CONFIG.SYS files), the less RAM is actually available to each DOS application. Common culprits are mouse drivers, network drivers, disk caches (like Windows SmartDrive) and so on.

To find out just how much memory is available to each DOS application, first start Windows. Then double-click the DOS icon to access the DOS prompt. At the prompt, type:

```
CHKDSK
```

This command displays several lines of information about your memory and disk space. The last line listing "bytes free" tells you how much memory is available to DOS applications.

*Warning* If you are using versions of DOS prior to 5.0, do *not* use the /F parameter with the CHKDSK command while in Windows. Outside Windows, this parameter assembles pieces of lost files into clusters you can examine and delete. Inside Windows, however, CHKDSK /F can cause you to lose data. Be sure to exit Windows before issuing this command at a DOS prompt.

49

## ▶ Load Windows first, TSRs next

> To increase memory for DOS applications, don't load memory-resident utilities from your AUTOEXEC.BAT. Instead, start Windows first; then launch a batch file to start the TSR utility.

When you launch a terminate-and-stay-resident (TSR) program before starting Windows, the TSR is available to the applications you run under Windows. Unfortunately, these memory-resident utilities rob some memory from each DOS application. The solution is to start Windows first, then load TSRs while inside Windows. For example, to use a DOS print spooler with Microsoft Word 5.0, save the commands for both in a batch file like this:

```
echo off
c:\utility\spool.exe
c:\word\word.exe
```

To launch this batch file, create an icon for it in Program Manager. When you double-click the icon, your spooler and word processor load with one quick step. The spooler will only be available to Word, but at least it won't take memory from other DOS apps. (If they need the spooler, create similar batch files for them.)

If you don't need to access your utility from inside a DOS application, you can launch it by itself from its own icon. The utility will appear in its own window while other applications are running.

So-called "pop-up" utilities can be run either alone or in a batch file with other DOS applications. The only difference is that when you're finished, you must press Ctrl-C to unload the utility from memory, as Windows will remind you (Figure 2-7).

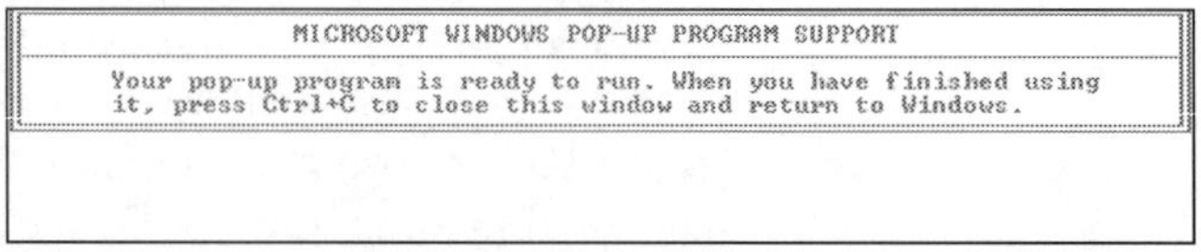

**Figure 2-7**
When you run a pop-up utility, Windows reminds you to press Ctrl-C to close the application.

```
MICROSOFT WINDOWS POP-UP PROGRAM SUPPORT
Your pop-up program is ready to run. When you have finished using
it, press Ctrl+C to close this window and return to Windows.
```

▶ **Note** If your utility has the file extension "SYS," you must launch it from your CONFIG.SYS file instead of inside Windows.

# DOING DOS

## ▶ Optimizing enhanced mode memory settings

> In 386 enhanced mode, use the KB Required and KB Desired settings for the minimum and maximum amounts of memory your application needs.

It's easy to be confused by the KB Required and KB Desired text boxes in your PIF Editor (386 enhanced mode) (Figure 2-8). Here are some tips to keep in mind:

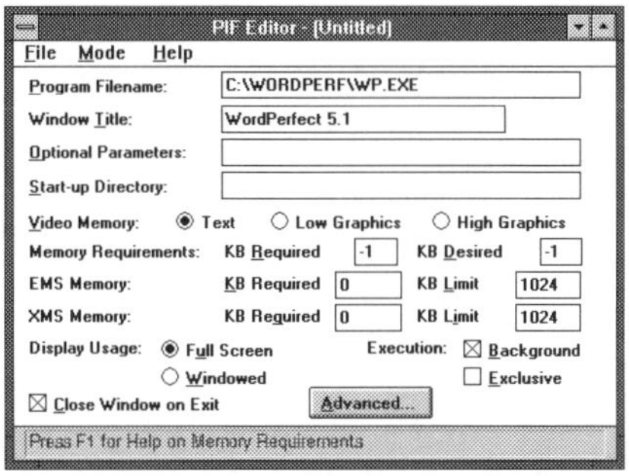

**Figure 2-8**
Entering a -1 in the KB Desired and KB Required boxes gives DOS applications the maximum amount of available conventional memory.

- Use the KB Required box for the *minimum* amount of RAM your DOS app needs. Enter an amount too small and your program may not load; too large, you may prevent Windows from using memory needed elsewhere. Start with 128K and experiment from there.

- Conduct your experiments with KB Required in standard mode so you can test your program in tight memory conditions.

- Use the KB Desired box for the *maximum* amount of memory your application will need. If it doesn't need a full 640K (the maximum), a lower amount will free up more memory for other apps.

- If your application is a RAM hog and runs better on more memory, enter -1 in both the KB Required and KB Desired text boxes. (If you enter -1 in the Required box, you *must* enter it in the Desired box.) This gives the app as much memory as Windows can scrounge up. Use this as a last resort; it wastes memory if the app doesn't really need it.

51

CHAPTER 2

## ▶ Maximizing RAM with upper memory blocks

> In 386 enhanced mode, you can increase the amount of memory available to each DOS application by using software (DOS 5.x, DR-DOS, 386Max, QEMM-386) that loads device drivers and TSRs into upper memory blocks.

On many computers, there is an under-utilized area of memory between your first 640K and 1024K. That 384K space is known as *upper memory blocks* or *UMBs*. Because it is normally used by your computer's hardware (such as your monitor), most programs cannot access UMBs. Consequently, you may have extra space up there that is going to waste.

If your computer can run in 386 enhanced mode, you can use special software to load device drivers (such as Windows' SMARTDRV.SYS) and other memory-resident utilities into upper memory blocks. The result is more conventional memory for each of your DOS applications. Several products have this capability, including:

- 386Max from Qualitas
- QEMM-386 from Quarterdeck
- DR-DOS from Digital Research
- MS-DOS 5.x from Microsoft

**Figure 2-9**
Software that manages your upper memory blocks (as shown on the right) can free more of your lower 640K for DOS applications.

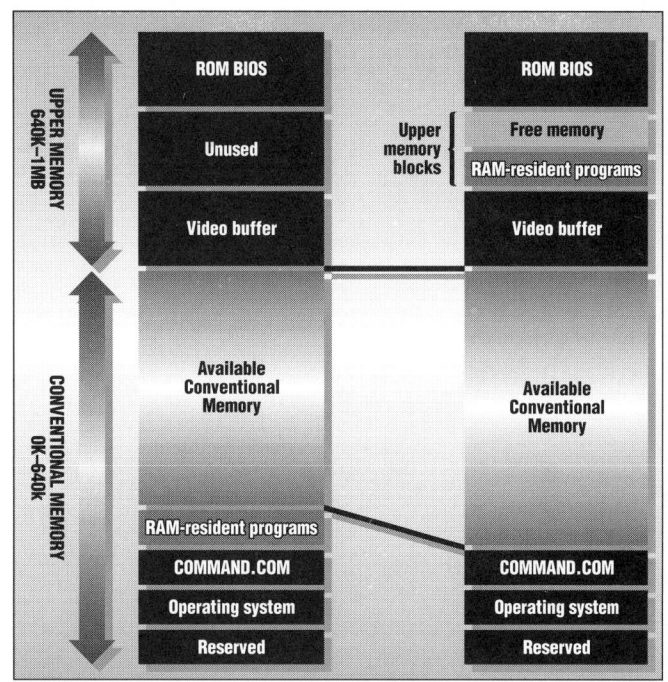

For details on using these products, refer to the documentation that comes with each.

CHAPTER 2

# DOS Dos and Don'ts

By now you may be getting the feeling that Windows is pretty much automatic and all you have to do is tweak it here and there to get the best results. While that is largely true, Windows isn't perfect. By making a few simple mistakes, you could do serious damage to some of your most important files.

This section will give you some basic advice about things you should *not* do to Windows, as well as things you can do to improve Windows treatment of DOS applications. You'll learn:

- Risky moves you should avoid
- How to protect your system from simple mistakes
- An alternate way to make your custom DOS icons appear on the desktop

## ▶ Avoiding the danger zone

> To avoid corrupting files, do not use any DOS program inside Windows that modifies your file allocation table — including disk compaction.

Certain DOS commands and programs should not be used from inside Windows at all, especially those that modify your hard disk's file allocation table. Be sure to exit Windows before using any of the software summarized below.

### Software to avoid while in Windows

| Software product or command | Explanation |
| --- | --- |
| CHKDSK /F | The /F parameter on this (pre-5.0) DOS command finds lost files and assembles them into a form you can examine and delete. CHKDSK by itself is fine, but using the /F parameter can cause loss of data. |
| Hard disk optimizing software (also called defragmenting or compaction software) | Such software can corrupt files on your hard disk, including files necessary to running Windows properly. |
| File undelete utilities | Unless your software specifically states that it is compatible with Windows 3.1, using such programs in Windows can corrupt disk files. |
| Hard disk back-up software | Crashes or lost data can result unless your backup software was designed with Windows 3.1 in mind. Check the program's documentation to be sure. |

## ▶ Overcoming DOS dangers

> If you wish to use defragmenting or other risky software inside Windows, either upgrade your software or buy the shareware Virtual 386 Write Protect Device.

If you're concerned that you or someone using your computer might use disk compaction, file undelete, or other risky software inside Windows (see previous tip), there is a solution, but it's not free. You may have to buy additional software.

### Upgrade your utilities
Many software companies, such as Central Point (makers of PC Tools) and Symantec (makers of the Norton Utilities) have released Windows and Windows-aware versions of their popular utilities. With them, it is now possible to safely back up disks and recover deleted files while in Windows.

### The Virtual 386 Write Protect Device
If you run in 386 enhanced mode, a cheaper alternative than upgrading all your utilities is to buy one small one — The Virtual 386 Write Protect Device from Mom's Software. This $20 shareware utility effectively "write protects" your hard disk while in Windows, preventing you from running CHKDSK/F, disk compaction (defragmenting) programs, accidental attempts to format your hard disk, and other disk writes not compatible with Windows. It also protects you from any virus that tries a similar maneuver. If you're the forgetful type, or simply want to protect your computer from novices, the Virtual 386 Write Protect Device is an inexpensive precaution.

## ▶ Custom DOS icons with other shells

> The shareware utility NoDOS lets you assign custom icons to your DOS applications that appear on the desktop when the application is minimized.

If you use Program Manager as your shell, you know that anytime you minimize an application (DOS or Windows), the icon appears on the desktop. But if you use File Manager or some other application as your shell, chances are that once you launch a DOS app and minimize it, the icon that appears on the desktop is the same old ugly default DOS icon. If you have several of these icons sitting on your desktop, you lose the value of graphical icons — you can't just click the picture that denotes your program; instead you must read the fine print below each icon to find the program you need.

NoDOS to the rescue! NoDOS is a $20 shareware utility that lets you assign your custom icons to your PIFs so they appear on your desktop whenever you minimize your application. NoDOS must be running in the background to make this magic work, where it takes up about 44K. But you set it to launch automatically from WIN.INI (see Chapter 1, "Blast Off.") and have its icon hidden by default, so you never know its there.

If you can spare the little bit of memory it takes, NoDOS gives DOS icons the functionality they deserve. And your desktop will look nicer, too.

For more information about changing Windows' shell, see Chapter 1, "Blast Off" and Chapter 5, "Custom Made Windows."

## ▶ Save time installing DOS applications

> To add multiple DOS applications to Program Manager in one swoop, use Windows' Setup utility. It automatically creates PIF files for most DOS apps. Setup stuffs the DOS apps in a group called Non-Windows Applications. Later, you can move your apps to different groups.

If you're only adding one new program, you can use ProgMan's New command on the File menu as explained in your *Microsoft Windows User's Guide*. But maybe you just downloaded a whole slew of apps from a BBS or a friend and you want to add them to Program Manager. Here's the best way to add multiple DOS applications.

When you first installed Windows, the Setup utility helped you add applications to Program Manager. Setup can help you do that same chore now as well. Just double-click Setup from your Main group. Then choose Set Up Applications from its Options menu. Direct it to search the drives of your choice. In a moment, it will present you with a list (admittedly imperfect) of the applications it finds on the designated drive(s). Select the items you want to add, click the Add button, then click OK (Figure 2-10).

**Figure 2-10**
Adding individual applications to Windows.

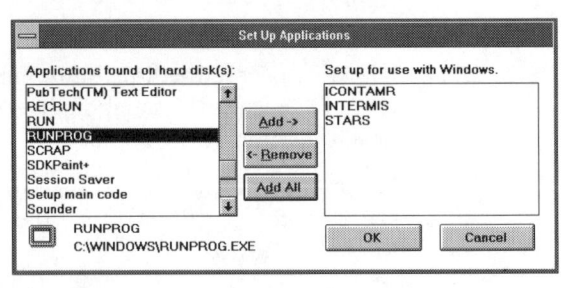

The good news is that Setup will automatically create PIFs for any DOS applications imported with this technique. The bad news is you can't designate what groups your apps are added to. DOS apps are automatically sent to the Non-Windows Applications group. You'll have to drag things around to get them where you want them.

# Summing Up

If you didn't know it before this chapter, you surely know it now: Windows isn't just for Windows. Armed with the tips you learned here, you can use Windows to multitask your DOS applications and have them running like a well-oiled machine. And you've learned how to improve their look and functionality too with a few key batch files and utilities.

In the next chapter, you'll learn how to continue Windows magic beyond your computer and onto the printed page. So stay tuned!

# CHAPTER 2

# 3 Prints Charming

**Simplifying printing and font handling**

In the not-so-olden days B.W. (before Windows), every bit of DOS software you installed had to have its own printer drivers. The installation routine gave you a list of ten zillion possible printers and you selected the right one to install.

Windows ended that with its device independence. The drivers that come with Windows work for all the programs that run under it. That's a big boon to Windows programmers. But it can help you, too, for the settings and accessories you use to get your work from computer to paper suffice for all the applications you use. It also means that the tips in this chapter will go a long way, improving all your Windows printing.

This chapter will help you streamline, simplify, and accelerate four main areas of printing:

- Font downloading
- Printing to disk
- Mastering PostScript
- Increasing speed and efficiency

# A-Fonting We Will Go

Once the realm of the lowly typesetter or desktop publishing specialist, fonts have become big business in the glitzy, graphical world of Windows. Windows 3.1 comes with scalable *TrueType* fonts. You can also buy *font rasterizers* from other companies. Our favorites are Adobe Type Manager, Bitstream FaceLift, and Zenographics Superprint.

This section explains how to get your soft fonts (those not built into your printer) from your hard disk to your laser printer. You'll learn the difference between manual and automatic downloading, when and how to do either, and the best ways to automate the whole process into utter effortlessness (just about).

## ▶ When to automatically download fonts

> To make the best use of printer memory and maximize speed, manually download your most frequently used fonts. Configure your least-used fonts for automatic downloading.

Your Windows applications know what fonts are built into your printer by looking in the printer driver — a file installed during setup. But with many laser printers, you can also use *soft fonts* that live on your hard disk rather than in the printer's ROM. To see them on the printed page, you must send (*download*) these fonts to the printer. The two most common methods are *automatic downloading* (fonts are sent to the printer only as needed for each page and immediately flushed out when the page is printed) and *manual downloading* (fonts are sent to the printers' memory, where they remain until the printer is turned off). Once a soft font is manually downloaded, it acts just like a resident font. Unfortunately, as soon as you turn off the printer, it "forgets" the soft fonts. They have to be downloaded again the next time you want to use them.

Automatic downloading only requires your attention once to set the fonts for auto-downloading. After that, it occurs invisibly. You can download as many fonts as you want (more or less), but printing is much slower.

Manual downloading requires a little effort from you each time the printer is turned on, but from then on printing is faster. The number of fonts you can download is limited by the amount of memory in your printer.

So which do you want? We advise manually downloading the fonts you use most often — like the font you use for your document's body text. That will speed things up. Reserve automatic downloading for fancy display faces that you seldom use or only use in occasional headlines. That way, you don't clog up the printer's memory with seldom-used fonts, and the oft-used fonts will print much faster.

# ▶ Downloading PostScript fonts automatically

> To make PostScript fonts download automatically, you must edit the [Postscript,Port] section of WIN.INI. To each *softfont* line, add a comma and the path of the font file.

If you use a PostScript laser printer, Windows provides no easy push-button way to download fonts manually or automatically. To set up fonts for automatic downloading, you have to edit the WIN.INI file in your Windows directory.

First, make a back up of WIN.INI in case you foul up. Next, find the section of WIN.INI that indicates your printer and port. The heading will be in brackets and will say something like [PostScript,LPT1]

Under that heading will be a list of your soft fonts, one line for each. For example, the line that references Helvetica-Black might read:

```
softfont1=C:\PSFONTS\PFM\HVBL____.PFM
```

To make a font auto-downloading, WIN.INI must list not only the PFM (printer font metric) file as shown in the example above. It must also list the actual font file, which usually has the .PFB extension (printer font binary). To do this, add a comma at the end of the line, no space, and the full path of the soft font file. The example below shows Helvetica-Black set for automatic downloading:

```
softfont1=C:\PSFONTS\PFM\HVBL____.PFM,C
:\PSFONTS\HVBL____.PFB
```

As you can see, all we've done is type in the name of the binary font file, so Windows can find it to download it.

Some font installation programs add this information during setup. Others just list the PFM file, which means the font must be manually downloaded. Now that you know the difference, you can make any soft font download the way you want.

# PRINTS CHARMING

## ➤ Downloading batch files for LaserJets

> You can use the Printer Font Installer dialog box to create batch files that download your favorite fonts. Just tell the Installer you want fonts downloaded at startup. Then remove the commands it inserts in your AUTOEXEC.BAT file.

Your Printer Font Installer dialog box (accessed through Control Panel) will let you download soft fonts to your HP LaserJet. You can also use it to create batch files for downloading different groups of fonts. That way, you can download fonts whenever you want — just by double-clicking an icon.

1. In Control Panel's Printer section, select your printer's name and click the Configure button. In the Printers - Configure dialog box, click the Setup button. In the next dialog box, click the Fonts button.

2. From the list of installed fonts on the left, select the ones you want for your batch file. Click the Permanent option button. (If you see a message box explaining "permanent" downloading, just click OK and continue.) The Download Options dialog box appears (Figure 3-1).

**Figure 3-1**
Choosing Download at startup creates a batch file you can use for font downloading.

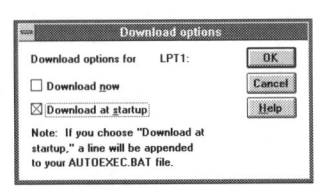

3. Make sure only the Download at startup box is checked. Then click OK. This creates a batch file in the same directory as your fonts and adds a line to your AUTOEXEC.BAT file.

4. Using a text editor like Notepad, open your AUTOEXEC.BAT file and locate the two lines added by the Font Installer dialog. They consist of a remark that reads, "rem The Windows PCL/HP Laser-Jet/DeskJet font installer added the next line," fol-

lowed by a line that executes the batch file. Make a note of the batch file's name, then delete both lines.

5. Repeat the above steps for as many different font groups as you want. Then create one icon for each batch file. (For more on assigning programs, PIFs, and batch files to icons, see Chapter 2, "Doing DOS.") To download your custom font group, just double-click on the icon of your choice.

## ▶ Downloading batch files for PostScript

> If you have the PCSEND utility from Adobe Systems, you can create batch files that download your favorite fonts to a laser printer on a parallel port. Create an icon for each batch file, and downloading becomes as easy as a mouse click.

All PostScript fonts from Adobe come with PCSEND, a utility for manually downloading fonts to a parallel printer. If your printer is connected to your computer's parallel port, you can use PCSEND to make font downloading double-click easy.

First, create a text file that contains the PCSEND commands for downloading the fonts you want. (Consult your PCSEND documentation for details.) The example below downloads Helvetica Condensed Black and Helvetica Condensed Black Oblique:

```
cd c:\psfonts
pcsend -1 -v hvcbl___.pfb
pcsend -1 -v hvco____.pfb
```

To dress them up further, use the DOS ECHO command to add comments that will appear on your screen. For example:

```
ECHO Now downloading Helv. Condensed Black
ECHO to the printer. Please wait...
```

Next, save the file with the .BAT extension. Finally, create an icon for the batch file in Program Manager (Figure 3-2). Each time you double-click the icon, your fonts are downloaded to your printer's memory. You can have different batch files for different groups of fonts.

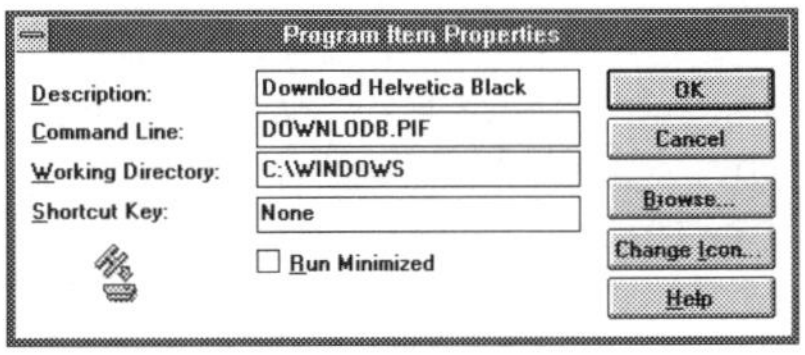

**Figure 3-2**
If you have an icon-drawing utility, you can create custom icons for each of your downloading batch files.

67

CHAPTER 3

## ▶ Smooth exits for downloading batches

> For optimum control of downloading batch files, create a PIF for each. In the PIF Editor, check Close Window on Exit if you want the batch file to return to Windows automatically; uncheck it to leave the batch file window open for you to read.

If you followed either of the two preceding tips, your batch files may either be executing and then disappearing before you read the screen messages, or the messages may stay on the screen, requiring manual labor to return to Windows. It all depends on the settings in your _DEFAULT.PIF file.

To control how your font-downloading batch files conclude, use the PIF Editor to create a PIF for each batch file, as instructed in your *Microsoft Windows User's Guide*. If you want to return to Windows immediately after downloading, check the Close Window on Exit box in the PIF Editor (Figure 3-3).

**Figure 3-3**
Use the Close Window on Exit box to control how your batch file concludes.

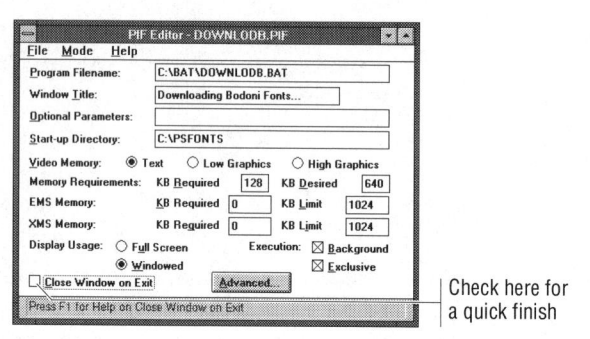

Check here for a quick finish

On the other hand, if you want the screen messages to remain visible until you've read them all, be sure the box is unchecked. In Windows standard mode, the batch file will conclude by prompting you to press any key to return to Windows. In 386 enhanced mode, you'll have to close the batch file window yourself by double-clicking its control menu box.

68

> **Hint** To make things even easier, check the Close Window on Exit box in your PIF, and add the following line to the end of your downloading batch file:

    pause

Now when you download fonts, the batch file will conclude with the message, "Strike a key when ready." Pressing any key closes the batch file window.

## ▶ Automating manual font downloading

> If you use batch files to manually download the same fonts each day, you can automate the process by adding the batch files to your AUTOEXEC.BAT. Just remember to turn on the printer *before* you turn on your computer.

Whether you have a PCL printer or a PostScript printer, you may find yourself downloading the same fonts every day. If you use batch files for manual font downloading, you can automate the process by adding those batch files to your AUTOEXEC.BAT. Then, each time you start your computer, the fonts will be sent to your printer without any fuss on your part.

For example, Figure 3-4 shows an AUTOEXEC.BAT file that downloads Adobe Garamond to the printer, then starts Windows:

**Figure 3-4**
For fonts you need every day, put your downloading batch files in AUTOEXEC.BAT.

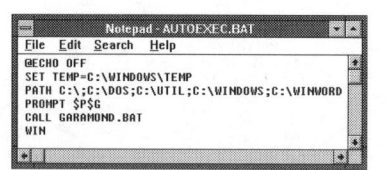

```
@ECHO OFF
SET TEMP=C:\WINDOWS\TEMP
PATH C:\;C:\DOS;C:\UTIL;C:\WINDOWS;C:\WINWORD
PROMPT $P$G
CALL GARAMOND.BAT
WIN
```

The only thing to remember is that you must turn on your printer before you turn on your computer. And, if you should turn off or restart or printer any time during the day, you will have to manually invoke your batch files to send the fonts to the printer again.

## ▶ Easier downloading with the Micrografx driver

*The Micrografx PostScript driver lets you download fonts automatically or manually easily from within Windows. The $199 utility also lets you control special printing effects.*

If you're annoyed at having to use a clumsy DOS utility (like PSDOWN) to manually download your PostScript fonts, or at having to edit WIN.INI every time you change a font from manual to automatic downloading, you're in luck. Micrografx, makers of the Windows drawing program Designer, have come up with a better PostScript driver for Windows, one that simplifies these and other printing chores.

The driver's easy-to-use dialog boxes (Figure 3-5) are accessed through Control Panel or the printer setup command of some applications. There you select from a list of your installed fonts and choose an option to download them manually immediately or designate them for auto-downloading when you print.

**Figure 3-5**
The Micrografx PostScript driver gives you point-and-click font downloading.

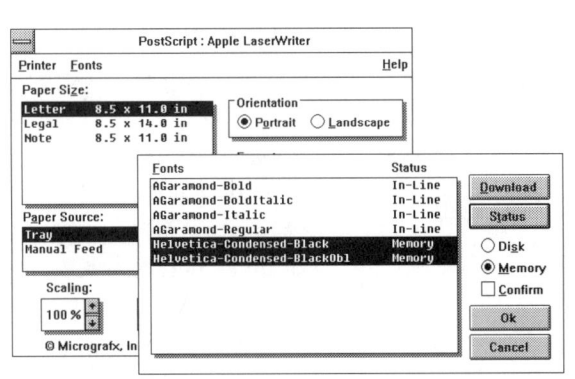

The driver also lets you control the default width of hairline rules if your Imagesetter draws lines that are too fine.

The driver comes with Designer but also sells as a separate product for $199.

## ▶ WinPSX for free and easy downloading

If you don't have PCSEND or PSDOWN, try the Windows freeware WinPSX from Costas Kitsos. It lets you download PostScript fonts to a printer through a dialog box or icon.

We saved the best font-downloading tip for last. If you use a PostScript printer, rush out to your favorite BBS or shareware trafficker and get Costas Kitsos's WinPSX — a *free* and full-featured PostScript font downloader for Windows (Figure 3-6).

**Figure 3-6**
WinPSX lets you download fonts with point-and-click ease.

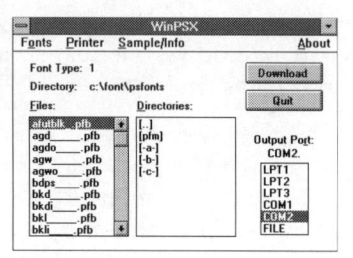

With WinPSX you can:

- Use the easy dialog box to point-and-click the fonts you want downloaded.

- Create custom font groups (or "JOB" files) for easy downloading of multiple fonts.

- Download a font group from an icon by entering WinPSX and a JOB file on your icon's command line.

- Associate JOB files (font groups) with WINPSX.EXE so that double-clicking a JOB file in File Manager downloads the group.

- Download selected fonts each time you start Windows (either by placing an icon in Program Manager's Start-Up group or by editing WIN.INI). For more information, see Chapter 1, "Blast Off."

Software this good has a habit of not staying free for long, so get it now. If there's a shareware fee by the time you read this, don't say we didn't warn you.

# Printing to Disk

Printing doesn't always mean getting your document to appear on paper. There are times when you want the print command to create a file — to export your document in a special format or to take the file elsewhere to be printed. For example, if you want your document printed on a typesetting machine but don't have $30,000 to spend on the hardware, you can simply make a print file. Then take the file to a service bureau, which will print it for a few dollars a page.

The process of making a print file is called *printing to disk* and it's available to all your Windows programs. This section tells you:

- How to use Control Panel to make a print file
- How to make a print file without the trouble of using Control Panel
- How to avoid naming the print file each time
- How to get automatic crop marks to print on a Linotronic typesetter

## ➤ How to make a print file

> To send printer output to a file on your disk (instead of to your printer), open the Printers section of Control Panel, click Connect, and designate FILE: as your port.

Sending printer data to a file instead of to your printer is easy in Windows. Here's the process:

1. First, open the Printers section of Windows' Control Panel.

2. In the list of Installed Printers, select the name of the printer whose format you'll use (for example, a PostScript printer to create a PostScript print file).

3. Next, click the Connect button.

4. In the Connect dialog box, scroll through the Ports list and select the word FILE: (Figure 3-7).

**Figure 3-7**
The Connect dialog lets you send printer information to a file.

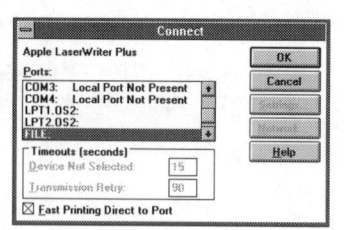

5. Click OK here and Close in the previous dialog. Close Control Panel.

6. Return to your application and print to the same printer you selected in Control Panel. You will be prompted for a filename. Be sure to write the complete path where you want the file stored on your disk.

## ▶ Printing to disk the easy way

> To simplify printing to disk, install your printer driver a second time. Assign one listing of the printer to your regular port and assign the other listing to "FILE:." You can then switch between each option from inside most applications.

The previous tip described the usual way to print to disk. Try that a few times and you'll tire of digging through dialog boxes just to make a print file. Instead, do this:

1. In Control Panel's Printers dialog box, click on Add Printer.

2. Scroll through the resulting list of printers until you find the name of your printer (never mind that it's already installed).

3. Click the Install button. Your printer's name appears a second time in the Installed Printers list.

4. With the new printer name selected, click Connect. Choose FILE: from the Ports list and click OK.

Now you won't have to go back to the Control Panel every time you want to print to disk. Just use your application's printer setup command to select the printer assigned to the computer port for regular printing, or select the printer assigned to FILE: for printing to disk.

## CHAPTER 3

> **Printing to an automatic filename**
>
> To print to disk without being prompted for a new filename each time, add the filename followed by an equal sign (=) to the [ports] section of WIN.INI. Then restart Windows.INI. Finally, open the Printers section, click Configure, and assign that filename as your printer's port.

If you only occasionally make print files, or only keep one print file on your hard disk at a time, you can save yourself the trouble of naming the print file each time you print to disk. You do so by creating a false "printer port" that is really a print file.

Here's how: open WIN.INI in an ASCII editor like Windows Notepad or System Editor. Then find the section with the heading [ports]. Under this heading, add a line with the filename you want to use followed by an equal sign (=). For example, you might add the following line:

```
printme.prn=
```

Now exit and restart Windows. Double-click the Printers section of Windows Control Panel. Click the Connect button and scroll through the list of ports. You'll see the filename you added in the list. Select it, click OK, then click Close and close Control Panel.

Now every time you print to this "port," Windows will create a print file by this name in your Windows directory. If you want the file to appear in another directory, add that path to the filename in WIN.INI.

**Warning** Each time you print to disk, the contents of the previous file are overwritten. Therefore, avoid this technique if you are likely to need more than one print file on your disk at a time or if others may be making print files on your computer.

## ▶ Use "Extra" sizes for Linotronic output

When printing automatic crop marks in a print file for Linotronic output, be sure to select one of the "Extra" sizes from the Paper Size list box in the printer setup dialog box.

Many desktop publishers make proof copies on a laser printer but make print files to send to a typesetter such as a Linotronic. Some programs, like PageMaker or Ventura for Windows, can print automatic crop marks on the typesetting paper to show the boundaries of your page when printed on the large rolls of paper that a Linotronic can use. But unless you take the proper steps, these crop marks may not show up.

The secret lies in the printer setup dialog box for the Linotronic. To open the dialog box, open the Printers section of Control Panel. Select the Linotronic printer that you assigned to the FILE: (or custom filename) port. (If you haven't installed a Linotronic printer driver, do so now with the Add button.) Click the Setup button.

▶ **Hint** Many apps, including PageMaker and Ventura for Windows, let you access the printer setup dialog box without going to Control Panel. Just look for a "Setup" button in the Print, Printer Setup, or Target Printer dialog boxes. You can also access this dialog from Print Manager (Printer Setup command, Options menu).

In the Paper Size list box, choose one of the "Extra" sizes — Letter Extra for letter-sized pages, Tabloid Extra for tabloid-sized pages, and so on (Figure 3-8). If you don't choose an "Extra" size, Windows won't print the crop marks.

**Figure 3-8**
When printing automatic crop marks, designate an Extra size for your Linotronic print file.

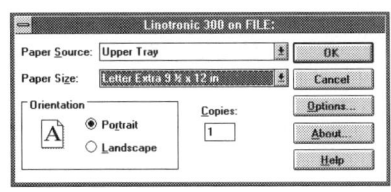

# Particularly PostScript

When it comes to high-quality laser printing and typesetting, PostScript is the standard. Not only is PostScript the language of many fonts, laser printers, and typesetting machines, but Encapsulated PostScript is also an important graphic file format. Because PostScript is so important, we've devoted this section to PostScript issues. But PostScript has a way of popping up in other contexts too, so be sure to read the rest of this chapter for additional PostScript hints.

This section will simplify your PostScript projects with the following tricks:

- Exporting any file to Encapsulated PostScript
- Speeding up print jobs by downloading the header only once
- Automating your header downloading
- Enabling your printer's error handler

## ➤ Universal exporting to EPS

> To export to Encapsulated PostScript when a Windows app doesn't give that option, install the Windows PostScript driver, open its setup dialog box, click Options, and select Print To: Encapsulated PostScript.

What if you want to export a graphic as Encapsulated PostScript but your application doesn't support that format? This is a problem with Excel, for instance, which can generate great graphic charts but has no EPS export option.

Here's your answer: first, if you haven't already done so, install the PostScript printer driver that comes with Windows. Next, open the PostScript setup dialog box from your application's Printer Setup command (or equivalent). Then click Options. In the Print To section, click the Encapsulated PostScript File option button (Figure 3-9). Then click OK and close the remaining dialog boxes.

**Figure 3-9**
The PostScript Options dialog turns your print command into an EPS export option.

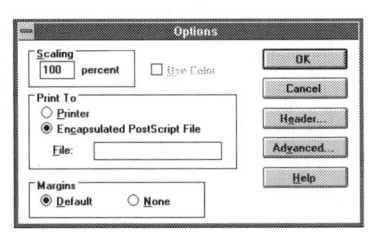

Now print to your PostScript driver, entering a filename (and path if desired) when prompted.

➤ **Hint** Don't enter a filename in the text box in the Options dialog box. The text box doesn't give you room for long pathnames and keeps the name in the dialog for the rest of your Windows session. Leaving it blank causes Windows to prompt you for the name each time you print. That prompt allows much longer path and filenames.

➤ **Hint** When trying this in Excel, first choose Page Setup from the File menu. Remove the header and footer text, set the margins to zero, and select Fit to Page.

# CHAPTER 3

### ▶ Speeding up PostScript printing

> If you send multiple print jobs to a PostScript printer each day, you can save time by sending the PostScript header information to a file and downloading that file only once each time the printer is turned on.

For all its wonders, PostScript is not exactly a speed demon at printing. However, if you send several jobs to your printer each day, you can shave some time off your PostScript printing under Windows.

First, open the PostScript setup dialog box either through Control Panel's Printers section or through your application. Then click Options button. In the Options dialog box, click Header. In the Header dialog box, click Download. In the Download Header dialog, select File and click OK (Figure 3-10).

**Figure 3-10**
You can speed up PostScript printing by making the header a file that is downloaded only once.

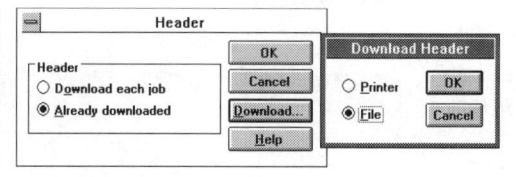

When prompted, type in the complete path and filename (30 characters maximum). Upon clicking OK, Windows creates a text file with the PostScript header information.

At this point you are returned to the Header dialog, where you should select Already downloaded. Then click OK and close all dialog boxes.

Finally, you must send the header file you created to your printer. You can use a downloading utility, such as PSDOWN or PCSEND, or you can use the DOS COPY command. The header will stay in your printer until the power is shut off. That means your application doesn't need to send it to the printer each time, saving you about 20 seconds per print job.

80

## ➤ Automating header downloading

> If you download a PostScript header to your printer only once a day, you can automate the process by putting the necessary command in your AUTOEXEC.BAT file. Just remember to turn on the printer before you turn on your computer.

The previous tip told you how to speed up printing by sending your PostScript header to your printer only once each day. You can automate that process even further by putting the download command in your AUTOEXEC.BAT file located in your root directory. That way, the chore is done automatically each time you turn on your computer.

If you use a utility like PCSEND to send the header to your printer, simply include that command in your AUTOEXEC.BAT file.

If your PostScript printer is connected to a serial port, you can't use the PCSEND utility. But you can still send the header to your printer with the DOS COPY command. For example, if you created the file HEADER.TXT in the Windows directory and have a PostScript printer on serial port COM1, the command you need looks like this:

```
copy c:\windows\header.txt com1:
```

Now all you have to do is add this line (or one like it) to your AUTOEXEC.BAT file.

*Warning* Whether you use the PCSEND utility or the DOS copy command, you need to turn on your printer *before* you turn on your computer. Otherwise, the AUTOEXEC.BAT will try in vain to send the header to a powerless printer.

## CHAPTER 3

> ### Making your printer report errors
>
> To enable your PostScript printer's error handler from within Windows, open the PostScript setup dialog box, click Options and click Advanced. Then check Use Error Handler. Click OK and close the other dialog boxes.

Sometimes your job won't print and you can't figure out why. Wouldn't it be great if your PostScript printer gave you an error message telling what went wrong? It can.

Open your PostScript setup dialog box through your application or through Control Panel's Printers section. Click the Options button and then the Advanced button. Make sure the Print PostScript Error Information check box is checked (Figure 3-11).

**Figure 3-11**
The Print PostScript Error Information check box tells your printer to print problem reports.

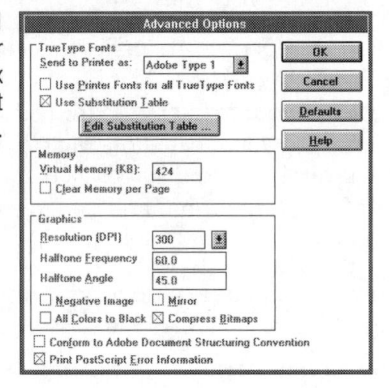

Click OK and close all dialog boxes. Now when your printer has a problem, it will print a sheet containing an error message. You may need some knowledge of PostScript to understand some of these messages, but it's better than nothing.

82

## ▶ Amazing grays

> To improve the gray tones of tint blocks in your document, open the PostScript setup dialog, click Options, then click Advanced. Set the Halftone Frequency number to 85 or 90.

A number of word-processing and desktop publishing apps (including PageMaker, Ventura Publisher, and Word for Windows 2.0) let you dress up your documents with gray tint patterns (like the one above). Your laser printer can't really print the color gray, of course, but it simulates the effect with black lines or dots placed close together. The problem is the default tint patterns on most laser printers produce coarse patterns whose obvious dots look, well, tacky.

But owners of PostScript printers are in luck. The PostScript driver included with Windows 3.1 lets you adjust the screen frequency and angle for better grays. Just open your PostScript setup dialog box through your application or through Control Panel's Printers section. Click the Options button and then the Advanced button. In the Advanced Options dialog box, try setting the halftone frequency to 85 or 90. Experiment until you find the best shades of gray for your document.

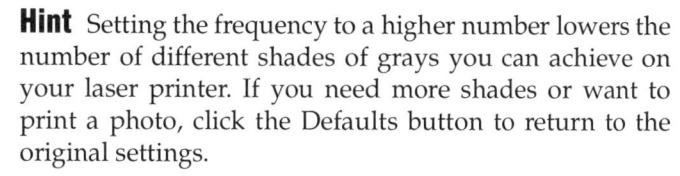

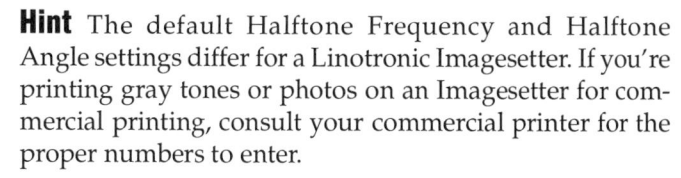

▶ **Hint** Setting the frequency to a higher number lowers the number of different shades of grays you can achieve on your laser printer. If you need more shades or want to print a photo, click the Defaults button to return to the original settings.

▶ **Hint** The default Halftone Frequency and Halftone Angle settings differ for a Linotronic Imagesetter. If you're printing gray tones or photos on an Imagesetter for commercial printing, consult your commercial printer for the proper numbers to enter.

# A Miscellany of Speed Tips

We've saved the best for last. This section gives you a handful of assorted tricks for improving printing speed and efficiency. You'll learn how to:

- Get quick text-only proof pages from your printer
- Optimize your use of Print Manager
- Get a better print manager like SuperQueue

PRINTS CHARMING

## ▶ Quick proofs with the Text Only driver

To get fast text-only output from a printer that supports ASCII, install and use the Generic/Text Only driver that comes on your Windows disks.

Because Windows is a graphical environment, many Windows apps send graphic information to your printer, which slows printing. But if you just want to see the text of a document, you can get speedy proofs by installing the Generic/Text Only driver that comes on your Windows disks. (Use Control Panel's Add Printer button shown in Figure 3-12 or see your *Microsoft Windows User's Guide*.)

**Figure 3-12**
Installing the Generic/Text Only driver can give you fast ASCII output.

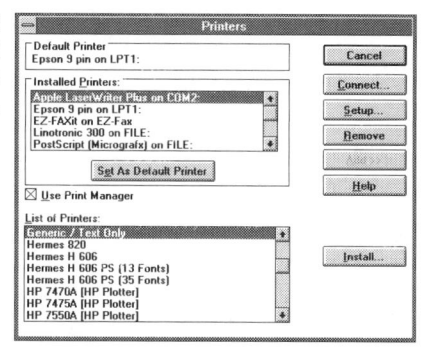

Designate the Generic/Text Only driver as the current printer in your application. As long as your printer supports ASCII, it'll print your document's text in no time.

The Generic/Text Only driver is a good way, for example, to get a proof copy of your Excel worksheet without waiting to print all the grid lines and boxes. The same goes for printing from Windows Cardfile, which otherwise draws boxes for each card. And if you print your output to a Generic/Text Only file, the info on your cards will be in an ASCII text file that you can edit. (For more information, see "Printing to Disk the Easy Way," on page 75.)

▶ **Hint** When printing Cardfile and Excel to an ASCII file with the Generic/Text Only driver, first open the Page Setup dialog box (File menu), and eliminate headers, footers, and margins.

## ▶ Managing Print Manager

> You don't have to accept the default settings of Print Manager. To change the effect it has on your multitasking or printing speed, adjust the settings in the Options menu or disable Print Manager altogether.

Print Manager is the print spooler that comes with Windows. It's not perfect, but it does let you return to your application faster than no spooler at all. To make sure you're getting the most out of Print Manager, consult the speed tips in the table below.

### Print Manager Speed Tips

| To accomplish this | Take this action |
| --- | --- |
| Get pages from the printer faster | Disable Print Manager: open Control Panel, double-click the Printers icon, uncheck the Use Print Manager box, and click Close |
| Return to the application faster after sending a job to the printer | Create a RAM drive with the RAMDrive utility that comes with Windows; then direct Windows temporary files to that drive as explained in your *User's Guide* |
| Get more speed in applications while printing in the background | Start Print Manager and choose Low Priority or Medium Priority from the Options menu |
| Get Print Manager to send pages to the printer as fast as possible | Start Print Manager and choose High Priority from the Options menu |

## ▶ Speeding up with SuperQueue

If you have a Hewlett-Packard printer, Zenographics Super-Print includes a superior print spooler called SuperQueue. It's faster than Print Manager and lets you delay printing to a more convenient time.

If Print Manager doesn't melt your butter, there are a few competing print spoolers available for Windows. Perhaps the best is SuperQueue, which comes with Zenographics' SuperPrint. SuperPrint includes support for numerous font technologies and a Print Manager replacement.

The bad news is SuperPrint only works with Hewlett-Packard printers such as the LaserJet or DeskJet. The good news is that if you have one of these printers, SuperPrint contains a whole collection of printing goodies — a font rasterizer that supports numerous font formats, a handful of scalable typefaces, and the print spooler, SuperQueue.

SuperQueue returns you to your application more quickly than Windows' own Print Manager. SuperQueue also lets you spool your print files to disk for later printing — at the end of the day, for example. If you have an HP printer, SuperPrint deserves your consideration.

# Summing Up

Computer journalists and other know-it-alls lump printers in a category known as *peripherals*. But while that term may have some technical accuracy, it connotes something of a secondary, or minor, importance. Yeah, right. Try telling that to anyone who has to get the spreadsheets ready for the board of directors, a newsletter out in time to meet a press deadline, or a term paper printed before the next class starts. No, printing is definitely not *peripheral*.

But if you apply the gimmicks you learned in this chapter, your next printing job may go just a little bit faster, require a little less work, and make a little more sense. If so, we've done our job.

In the next chapter, we'll tackle the more global task of optimizing the way Windows fits into your entire computing system—RAM, hard disk space, and special shortcuts the pros use. When you get through, you'll be more of a pro yourself.

# 4 Optimizing your System

**Managing memory, disk space, and resources for maximum power**

Windows' installation routine has set the standard for what such a program should do. With a single typed command, wisely dubbed Setup, Windows is configured to suit your system. Still, there are many steps you can take to make the environment faster and more powerful.

This chapter will discuss how to tweak both hardware and software for maximum efficiency. Pretty soon, you may be able to emulate Scotty on *Star Trek*: able to push the system to its limits and fix any problem with a couple of whacks in the right place.

# Jogging the Memory

When discussing the Windows advantage, the most significant aspect is always memory. With DOS, users were always mindful of the 640K limit — the digital equivalent of a barbed wire fence. Windows snips the fence and lets you out into the RAM pasture. Once you've used Windows for a while, the magic number *640* will rarely enter your mind.

Windows memory management, however, isn't quite effortless. Once out in the pasture, you may discover there's bugs in them thar hills. Some ways to load up on the bug spray:

- Buy more memory (the ever-popular solution)
- Delete the contents of the Clipboard when you're done with them
- Don't bother with Windows wallpaper
- Watch your available system resources
- Dump unused utilities and drivers from CONFIG.SYS and AUTOEXEC.BAT
- Use a utility to monitor your memory usage

## OPTIMIZING YOUR SYSTEM

### ➤ Get more

> Adding more RAM is frequently the most effective way to improving your memory management. Jumping from 2MB to 4MB of RAM can double your processing power.

OK, this is an obvious tip, but it's still important to remind you that the simplest way to supercharge Windows is to buy more memory. There are those who have proposed adding a warning dialog box to the Windows system. When applications get sluggish, it pops up and announces "Time to buy more memory!"

While the amount of memory you need to run Windows depends on applications (desktop publishing, for instance, is one of the most memory intensive and should not be attempted with less than 4 MB of RAM) there is one general rule: 2 MB, the standard level for most new machines, will be adequate only if you don't try to run more than one or two applications simultaneously.

The jump between 2 MB and 4 MB is one of the most perceptible hardware upgrades, similar to moving to a PC AT after using a sluggish XT. All at once, everything moves at a reasonable speed. The Windows become unfogged. The upgrade can often cost less than $200 and can be accomplished by just plugging chips into the motherboard.

4MB should be enough for ordinary users. But if you run lots of applications at the same time, or if you use graphics intensive applications like desktop publishing or drawing programs, you may want to go to 8MB or beyond.

## ▶ Clear the Clipboard

**Clearing the Clipboard once you've pasted the Clipboard's contents can free large amounts of memory.**

Windows' Clipboard is an application that you may never load on its own, but it's one that you're guaranteed to use all the time. In simplest terms, the Clipboard is a cut-and-paste tool. It always contains the last item that was cut using the Cut or Copy commands from your application's Edit menu (Figure 4-1).

When you put something on the clipboard, it stays there until you replace it with something else or clear it out manually. What kinds of things eat memory? Long text files, anything in color, and any kind of bitmap. If you've loaded the clipboard with a memory hog, you may want to take a moment to flush it out of the system, especially if you're operating with a 2MB machine. To do so:

1. Open the Clipboard by double-clicking its icon (usually in the Accessories group).
2. Select Delete from the Edit menu.
3. Exit the Clipboard.

**Figure 4-1**
Purging the Clipboard is one way to save memory.

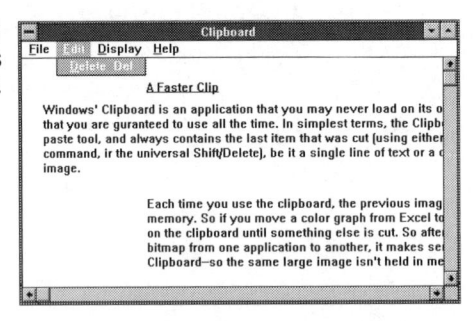

## ▶ Scrape off the wallpaper

*Wallpaper is pretty, but it uses valuable system resources you may not have.*

Wallpaper, the ability to decorate the onscreen desktop with scanned bitmaps or color images, is one of the most dramatic — and wasteful — parts of Windows' appearance. Holding a color image in memory can take 60K or more of memory, the equivalent of covering part of your central workspace with a useless (although pretty) bauble. In addition, the wallpaper consumes part of Windows' precious system resources, a separate segment of memory set aside to manage the user interface (see the previous tip).

It's fun to have a picture of Elvis visible at all times. On the other hand, most offices put art on the walls and leave the desks clear for getting work done. And so should you if you're working with a 2MB machine, or if you often run low on system resources.

CHAPTER 4

## ▶ Resource conservation

> Another good way to conserve system resources is by eliminating unneeded icons and program groups and closing applications when you're done with them.

There are two types of Windows memory, both of which need to be conserved. But if standard memory is moody, the more precious system resource memory is downright temperamental. Due to Windows' disk swapping abilities, the amount of standard memory is practically infinite (although swapping to disk does slow things down quite a bit.)

System resource memory, on the other hand, is very limited, with every little thing from an icon to a menu taking a bite. This represents the standard tradeoff between looks and efficiency: many of the most resource-hungry aspects are visually oriented. So you actually allow the system to run better by making it less pretty.

You can get an idea of available system resources by switching to Program Manager and choosing About from the Help menu (Figure #]-2). To see how it works, check system resources when you start up Windows. Then open two or three programs and check system resources after each one. Finally, try opening a half dozen group windows in Program Manager and checking again.

**Figure 4-2**
Even with plenty of RAM available, resources may be low.

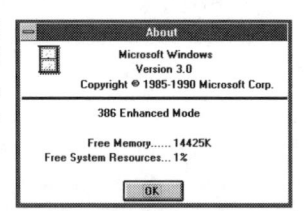

About
Microsoft Windows
Version 3.0
Copyright © 1985-1990 Microsoft Corp.
386 Enhanced Mode
Free Memory.......14425K
Free System Resources... 1%
OK

See how easy it is to gobble up system resources just by opening programs and windows? Most people report that they start to experience crashes and other problems when system resources get below 25 percent.

If you're not running into any trouble, you may not need to worry about system resources. On the other hand, if

## OPTIMIZING YOUR SYSTEM

you're running into lots of unexplained crashes, you may want to try one or more of these resource-saving tips:

*Minimize the use of icons.* Custom-designed Program Manager icons sure are cool, but they burn fuel. It's tempting to get carried away, developing icon links for every active file, but this kind of fast living can cause an early death. Only install icons for programs that you need or use regularly. For the stuff you use only once a month, load them through Program Manager's "Run" command.

*Consolidate program groups.* If you have a lot of programs, it's also tempting to establish a group for every category or project. Again, you should only keep groups that make consistent sense — having a group with only one or two icons is an unnecessary waste. Program groups, however, only take resources when they are open — that is to say, when the icons are visible on the desktop. If you minimize a group onto the desktop, it represents no resource drain.

Keeping down the number of groups can be a constant struggle, as many application programs create their own program groups at installation. Norton Desktop for Windows is perhaps a good example. It creates its own program group with about 15 different icons. After this point, you should delete icons for the programs you'll rarely use and combine the remainder with another group. The savings will be substantial.

*Close applications not in use.* Unlike program groups, applications continue to draw resources even when they are minimized. So if you're running Word for Windows with an active ribbon, ruler, and scroll bar, this drain continues even if the application is in icon form. The answer is to close the program during any prolonged period of inactivity.

The second part of this solution has to do with the program itself. When possible, close its optional visual aspects. For instance, many word processors have horizontal scroll bars. Most writers find this feature about as useful as a second set of tonsils. Also, rulers, ribbons, icons, and menus should all be kept to a minimum. To accomplish this, most programs allow you to streamline visuals underneath the "Preferences" menu.

## ▶ Start with a clean slate

> Remove unused drivers and programs from CONFIG.SYS and AUTOEXEC.BAT to free more memory.

The more memory you have when starting Windows, the more memory it can use. This isn't a difficult concept. Windows' memory management may be smart, but it can't repossess blocks of memory that are claimed by another program. The solution is to make sure that all possible memory is available to Windows at startup, and the best way to do this is to delete all unnecessary memory drains from the system.

To streamline memory usage, you must cut the chaff from CONFIG.SYS and AUTOEXEC.BAT, the files used during startup. First — and of extreme importance — back up these files. Then, open each with a text editor and examine each line to determine its importance. Delete the obviously unnecessary, but don't delete commands about which there is any doubt. For instance, remove any command that loads protocols for a program that you no longer use, but be more careful about deleting what appears to be incomprehensible gibberish (it's always more important than it looks). Streamlining these files has the potential to free up quite a bit of memory.

## OPTIMIZING YOUR SYSTEM

### ▶ Know what you have

Memory monitors, such as hDC's Memory Viewer, can tell you where the memory is going.

You can always find out exactly how much free memory is in your system from the Program Manager (click About from the Help menu). In reality, this tells you almost nothing, like a movie review that begins and ends with the information that it was filmed in Chicago.

To manage memory with any efficiency, you need something with a little more power, such as hDC's Memory Viewer (Figure 4-3). Once only available as part of the company's FirstApps package, this little utility found a new home as part of Microsoft's $14.95 Resource Toolkit. By clicking on the Control Box (the little grey square in the upper left-hand corner of every window) you can get a graphical presentation of how memory is currently being used in your system, breaking down exactly how much RAM is used by each application.

Memory Viewer is essential for anyone who needs to know more about memory than the gross amount — actually, anyone who wants to use it to any advantage. If the system slows down you can figure out exactly which application is the memory hog, instead of deleting stuff at random in the hope that you make the right choice.

**Figure 4-3**
hDC's Memory Viewer gives an honest RAM breakdown.

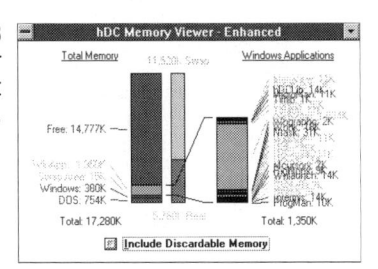

CHAPTER 4

# Driving that Disk

When Windows first arrived, Microsoft maintained Windows could operate on an XT-class machine with floppy drives. Both these myths are now thankfully abandoned. But a hard disk doesn't mean *any* hard disk, nor can any aspect of mass storage be taken for granted. Some helpful tips are:

- Buy a new hard disk to replace your older, slower hard disk

- Eliminate useless or unused programs and files to increase free space on the disk

- Defragment the disk to consolidate available space

## Mini Review: The Resource Toolkit

Everyone can use help with Windows on some level. For that reason, Microsoft's $14.95 Resource Toolkit is an outstanding bargain. Published unpretentiously in a loose-leaf binder, it provides tips, tricks, advice, and software for beginners and power users alike. With sections on installation, memory management, and running DOS applications under Windows, everyone will find some way to fine-tune their Windows system that will make it worth the price.

The software in the package is a bizarre mix. In addition to hDC's essential Memory Viewer, it also includes an icon design program, a troubleshooting package, and a program to create and design fish for a screen saver.

## ▶ Replace it

> Replacing your old hard disk with a newer, faster one can double or triple the speed of swapping between applications.

Along with boosting your memory above the 3 MB mark, replacing your hard disk with a newer, faster model can offer the most noticeable speed upgrade for the system as a whole. While this isn't as universal as the RAM boost, it will help in situations where your application is *disk intensive* (where it reads and writes alot). Also, if you run with *virtual memory* to any great extent (where hard disk space is used as RAM), speed is of the essence.

The rule is the same with any car or hard disk: the faster, the better. In Windows' case, hardware jocks recommend that the disk have an access time faster than 20 milliseconds (the smaller the number, the faster the disk). Although there are many fine disks that run at 28 milliseconds, this may not be quite good enough for a Windows user.

Replacing a drive in an existing system is a little more costly and complicated than adding RAM. Unless the drive is on an expansion card, adding a drive probably isn't something you'll want to try alone. So while upgrading a drive for speed, it also makes sense to increase the capacity. If you intend to use several Windows applications or have a need to store graphics or bitmaps, you'll want a disk capacity between 100 and 200 MB. If this seems like a lot at first, it won't after a while — especially when you take into account that a scanned photograph can occupy 1 MB or more of disk space.

## ▶ Clean it

> Periodically scouring your hard disk for unused and outdated files and programs is like taking out the trash frequently: you'll have a lot more room to work.

Depending on configuration, the Windows system itself takes about 5 MB of hard disk space, while most Windows applications will take at least 1 to 3 MB each. (Word for Windows 2.0, for example, takes 15 MB if you install everything!) Add data files and utilities, and a 40 MB disk that once seemed like a wide open prairie will feel like part of the Lower East Side.

Although we preach the 200 MB gospel, you can actually survive with much less. Chances are you can even save 1 MB right away, without leaving your chair, by disposing of system utilities you don't really need.

The first things to consider dumping are the Help files. Windows itself isn't all that hard to use. Once you've mastered the basics, you may never need Help again.

All Windows help files are conveniently recognizable by their HLP suffix. Consider erasing the Help files that are tied to never-used or well-known applications. Getting rid of the Word for Windows help file (and really, how complicated is Word for Windows?) will save half a megabyte. But don't delete the Windows help engine (WINHELP.EXE). You may need it for new applications.

The second type of dispensable Windows file is the "applet," the demonstration Windows applications that are automatically installed with the system. There are three reasons you may want to dump these programs:

- **They're useless.** Clock and Calendar add little beyond showing what a graphical interface can do. Watching a clock tick by is a waste of time and space, especially since most people who own PCs have watches as well.

- **They're redundant.** If you have a full-featured word processor, communications program, macro utility, or drawing package, there will be little need to retain

# OPTIMIZING YOUR SYSTEM

Windows' Write, Terminal, Recorder, or Paintbrush. Any plain ASCII editor makes Notepad superfluous.

- **They're bulky.** If you were to dump most of the applets, you'd save about 1 MB of disk space.

Applets are easy to identify because they have an identifying name plus the EXE extension. Notepad, for instance, is NOTEPAD.EXE.

**Warning** If you're getting rid of applets to save space, make sure you don't delete necessary Windows systems applications such as Clipboard, Progman, or PrintMan — all of which have the standard .EXE suffix, and reside in the Windows directory.

There are some other minor tricks you can use to save bytes. For one thing, you can eliminate all of the unnecessary .BMP (bitmap) files from your system. CHESS.BMP may be fun, but it serves little useful purpose. You can also add a line to your AUTOEXEC.BAT file:

```
DELETE C:\TEMP\*.*
```

to clean out the temporary directory each time you boot.

Finally, as a last resort, you can consider removing the games that came with Windows. But you probably shouldn't do this unless you're really tight for space.

**Note** If you're just not sure if you're going to need something or not, you can use a compression utility such as PKZIP from PKWare to compress your unused files. Files compress anywhere from 10-20 percent for .EXE files, to 40-60 percent for .TXT and .DOC files, to 93-97 percent (!) for .BMP files. If it turns out you need to use a file you compressed, you can run PKUNZIP to decompress the file in a matter of seconds.

## CHAPTER 4

### ▶ Defragment it

> The data on your hard disk can become *fragmented* (spread out), slowing access time. Regularly defragmenting the hard disk keeps all the data in contiguous files that are faster to access.

As part of daily use, data may be spread all about the four corners of a hard disk. For this reason, you should regularly run a defragmentation utility, which automatically reallocates spare bits closer to the data center. Since this brings all parts of the file to one place, it will improve performance, save file load time, and give your hard disk a longer life. But be careful out there — many defragmentation utilities need to run when Windows isn't active, or serious data damage can result.

# Take It on the Road

As more and more of us become hungry for Windows productivity, there emerges the desire to order it "to-go." While laptops have always required a power compromise, there is a new portable subcategory that can run Windows with relative ease — relative, because there are a few things you need to consider if you plan to use a new laptop for Windows, such as:

- Which best processor chip to use
- How to squeeze the most from your RAM and hard disk space
- What kind of pointing device to use

## ▶ The right processor

> Although 286-based laptops and notebooks are pretty cheap, you'd be better off buying one with a 386 chip.

Laptops and notebooks based on the 286 processor are getting cheaper and cheaper. Pretty soon they'll be so inexpensive you won't need to get permission from your boss or your spouse to buy one. Still, if you plan to use Windows for more than taking notes or checking e-mail, these machines are a bad choice. A wiser purchase is a machine with a 386SX or 386 processor. Speed aside, the most important aspect is the ability to run in enhanced mode.

## OPTIMIZING YOUR SYSTEM

### ▶ Maximize RAM and hard disk space

You'll do best running Windows on a laptop when you don't overload the machine's capabilities.

This is, of course, true with any computer you might buy for use with Windows. You don't want anything with less than 4 MB of RAM or a 40 MB hard disk... no, make that 60. Too many laptops, however, are cursed with 20 MB hard disks (which are, incidentally, slower than molasses). The problem with laptops is that upgrades are expensive. So get it right the first time. If you're buying a new laptop for Windows, make sure it has enough power to get around the first lap.

It's possible to run Windows on a 20 MB notebook, once you boil your needs down to the absolute essentials. You should, however, avoid the temptation to use Stacker or any other data compression utility to try to stretch the space into something it isn't. The generally slow laptop hard disk will suffer from the one-two punch of handling Windows and the compression program at the same time. So, you may input a command that doesn't execute until the next lunar cycle.

## ▶ Get the point(ing device)

*It's tough using a mouse on a plane or in a car. Learn the keyboard equivalents and look into trackball or "ballpoint" mice that clip to the side of the computer.*

Using Windows without a mouse builds character. You're forced to use and memorize keyboard commands. The first time you try to play Solitaire on the road, however, the mouseless PC will be the recipient of untold curses. To solve this, trackball-driven laptop pointing devices are available from companies such as Logitech and Microsoft. Respectively, the TrackMan Portable and the Ballpoint Mouse attach to the laptop's side or front and are controlled with a rolling thumb motion.

Considering the competition between the two companies and the independent development effort, the Logitech and Microsoft products are remarkably similar — right down to their $175 list price. Both have configurable buttons and can be detached from the bracket for use on a leg or other odd surface. Logitech, however, boasts a smaller, more comfortable ball and a sturdier bracket.

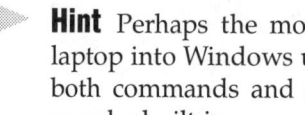

▶ **Hint** Perhaps the most important aspect of pressing a laptop into Windows use is having enough I/O ports for both commands and communication. One or the other may be built in, as an increasing amount of new laptops have either a mouse port or a pre-installed modem. Unfortunately, some have just one serial port. If you want to get any use out of portable Windows, this is an unacceptable situation — being one port short is another way to lose either your mind or your hair.

# The Thrill of Acceleration

While we've made a lot of compromises to use our personal computers, these concessions are fast disappearing. One is speed. A computer can never be too fast, and once you've achieved a certain velocity, it's quite unacceptable to regress. This is perhaps most apparent with word processing. If you've ever used XyWrite or DOS-based MS Word, using Word for Windows may remind you of taking your pet snail for a walk. Some speed-enhancing possibilities are:

- Using a permanent swap file on your hard disk
- Tune SMARTDrive
- Replace SMARTDrive with HyperDrive
- Run in standard mode
- Add a RAM drive

## CHAPTER 4

## ▶ Use a permanent swap file

> Windows can set up a permanent swap file on the hard disk, so it knows where to look when it swaps information.

When running in enhanced mode, Windows swaps to hard disk, trading this memory as if it were installed RAM. This greatly expands the parameters of the system. In its default mode, Windows creates a swap file on the fly. You can further increase speed by creating a permanent swap file. This contiguous portion of your hard disk is allocated for Windows' exclusive use.

To create such a file, you must:

1. Start Windows.

2. Start Control Panel.

3. Select the 386 Enhanced icon.

4. Select the Virtual Memory button from the 386 Enhanced dialog box.

5. Use the recommended settings in the Virtual Memory dialog box, or enter your own specifications. Click OK when you're satisfied.

This procedure sets up a hidden swap file that can only be used by Windows, so you're essentially eliminating disk space for use by data or other applications. For this reason, you should only allocate an amount of hard disk space that you can comfortably sacrifice.

You can change the size of the swapfile at any time with the same procedure.

## ▶ A smarter SMARTDrive

> SMARTDrive is a good product, but tuning it for your system can frequently make it better.

Windows is fairly disk intensive, making frequent calls to the hard drive. This slows down the system, causes wear on the hard disk, and, in portable systems, represents a battery drain. To alleviate this, Windows contains SMARTDrive, a disk caching program that holds the most recent information in RAM, so the system doesn't have to refer to the disk to load it again.

Windows probably installed SMARTDrive for you during initial setup. If you've added memory since then, or if you notice that the disk drive light is on too often, consider increasing the amount of memory allocated to SMARTDrive. To do this, you need to add a statement to your CONFIG.SYS file, using Notepad or another ASCII text editor. Determining the size to use for the cache will be a process of trial and error, depending on the applications you use and the memory they need. While fine tuning will be necessary, one place to start is the allocation of ¼ of your installed RAM to a cache. For example, if you have a 4 MB machine, add the following command to your CONFIG.SYS file (the second number determines the minimum size of the cache):

```
device=C:\windows smartdrv.sys 1024 256
```

## ➤ Or no SMARTDrive at all

> HyperDisk is a good replacement for SMARTDrive, particularly if you usually do just a couple of things with your computer.

For a truely fine-tuned system, you can replace SMARTDrive with a more versatile disk-caching program. For instance, HyperDisk is a $69 utility that caches in conventional, extended, or expanded memory. Not only does it have a more straightforward installation program — you don't need to mess with CONFIG.SYS. It places data from both the user and the disk into the buffer. If you're a predictable user and run the same routines over and over — like most people — HyperDisk can visibly increase performance.

## ▶ Standard behavior

> Running in standard mode is a good way to speed up Windows, but only if you're going to use one application at a time.

A straightforward way to increase Windows' speed is to run in standard mode. This option is the only way to run on a 286-based machine. But if speed is of the essence, you can also use standard mode on a 386.

In standard mode, you sacrifice the ability to create virtual machines or substitute hard disk space for RAM. In this case, the machine uses only the RAM that is physically installed. However, this memory is by nature faster, since no disk action is required. You won't be able to run DOS applications in a window, but for the most part, operating in standard mode has little or no effect on most Windows programs — it just lets them run a little faster, because Windows has to spend less time on system overhead.

To enter standard mode, use win/s as the start command.

CHAPTER 4

## ➤ Ewe need a RAM drive

> A RAM drive uses extra RAM to simulate a hard disk that operates at RAM speed. This is the best of both worlds if you have a lot of RAM in your computer.

Windows' little bag of driver tricks includes a utility to create a RAM drive — essentially a logical disk drive built from memory. In some cases, a disk cache will be a smarter use for extra RAM, but a RAM drive can provide a good place to temporarily store data for fast retrieval.

Like SMARTDRV.SYS program (Windows' disk cache), RAMDRIVE.SYS is installed into the CONFIG.SYS file. If you wanted to allocate 256K for a RAM drive, for instance, you would type the line

    device= c:\windows\ramdrive.sys 256

somewhere below the line containing the HIMEM.SYS command in CONFIG.SYS file.

The use of RAM drives sometimes make sense if you have at least 8MB of memory and you use programs, such as CorelDRAW and PageMaker, that make extensive use of temporary disk files. By setting the system so those temporary files are written to and read from the RAM disk, you can speed up operation.

To relocate the temporary files, you edit CONFIG.SYS. Make the TEMP variable point to the RAM drive. For instance, if CONFIG.SYS currently has a line that reads:

    SET TEMP=C:\TEMP

you would change it to read:

    SET TEMP=D:

if D: was the letter you assigned to the RAM drive.

The most important thing to remember about RAM drives is their volatility. You need to take the extra step of saving everything to a real hard disk before exiting. Remember, if the power goes, the data does, too.

# The Agony of Defeat

To a great extent, a Windows user is at the mercy of the system. For one thing, you can only select from the choices that are offered. You can always reboot, but that's akin to cheating (and it can be dangerous if data is at stake). Although you need to place your faith in Windows, there are a few ways to ensure that your computing life is accident-free:

- Prevent unrecoverable application errors (UAEs)
- Know how to rebuild your program groups
- Avoid disaster by backing up regularly
- If nothing else works, "punt" — reboot the computer and try again

## Fighting terrorism

> Unrecoverable application errors (UAEs) are the bane of Windows programs. Here's how to prevent them.

The worst part of using Windows is trying an operation and being suddenly greeted by a big white box that warns of an "Unrecoverable Application Error." Windows users have become so well acquainted with these little nasties they have awarded them a nickname: UAE. These initials strike fear into the hearts of every Windows user, and rightly so; UAE sounds like a government agency.

The simple explanation for UAEs is that they're caused by memory conflicts, when two programs argue over the same memory segment. The loser suffers the UAE and is removed from memory. In theory, the offending application leaves the scene quietly, with no effect on the other active programs. Reality, however, is not so predictable. If you get a UAE and click OK, there is no assurance of what will happen. The UAE'd application may slink to the sidelines quietly (like it's supposed to), the system may freeze, or it may even reboot. Your data may or may not survive a UAE (good luck).

Some of the things that to cause UAEs (aside from the ever-popular-but-nebulous "buggy software") are:

- Running the incorrect DOS version for your system
- Using software designed for a past Windows version
- An error in setup
- Incompatible memory resident software
- Page mapping conflicts in upper memory

The best cure is prevention. The wisest preventive action is a tip listed earlier, streamlining your AUTOEXEC.BAT and CONFIG.SYS files to eliminate useless commands. In this respect, you want to stay as close to "normal" as possible, avoiding exotic drivers, unconventional memory resident software, and bizarre disk-partitioning utilities. See Chapter 2, "Doing DOS," for information on cleaning up your system files.

## ▶ Return and regroup

> You can rebuild the program groups if they get messed up by running the Windows SETUP program again.

Less drastic — but just as annoying — is when bad things happen to good program groups. This corruption can be fixed automatically from within the Program Manager, choose File Run. Then type Setup/P in the dialog box.

Windows will rebuild your groups. The bad news is that the groups are rebuilt using the default Windows icons. And if you had attached custom icons, you'll have to re-install them separately.

## ▶ Backing up is hard to do

> Nobody likes backing up their computer, but you're going to lose data some day if you don't.

Backing up your data and files is a pain. Feeding floppy diskettes to the computer takes quite a while, even hours if you have a very large hard disk. A tape drive is quick and easy, but they still cost $250 and up and aren't very popular with home users.

Nevertheless, you have to back up your hard disk regularly. For example, the previous tip told you how to rebuild your program groups. If you simply restored from a backup, you wouldn't have to re-install custom icons; you'd just restore them from a backup.

There are grimmer things that can happen, too. Viruses that destroy hard disks intentionally are becoming more common. And even if you never get disks from anyone else, hard disks don't last forever. A hard disk failure can destroy all the data on the disk — Zip! <squeeeeeeeeeek>. All gone, just like that. Programs are relatively easy to replace, but your data isn't.

Back up your data frequently: weekly if you use the computer for an hour or two a day, daily if you use it more. If you're in a hot and heavy work session, you might want to save key files to a diskette every hour or so just in case. Do a complete backup of everything at least once a month — sure, you could restore the programs from the original diskettes, but it would be a nuisance to set them up and reconfigure them. Save your backups for at least six months. You never know when you're going to need that one stray file you created last October.

There are any number of good backup programs on the market, such as Central Point Software's PC Tools Deluxe. If you don't want to spend money on backup software, you can always use the BACKUP utility that comes with DOS. With BACKUP, you'll limp rather than run, but it works well enough to get the job done.

## ▶ When all else fails, reboot

Restarting your computer is drastic, but it may be the best way to clean out your RAM and start over.

Windows isn't a perfect system, nor is its behavior always logical. If it's acting unruly, there may be no other option but to clean the field and start over. A UAE will usually allow you to save and exit without losing data, and, in many cases, a simple reboot will get rid of the "slows..." at least temporarily.

CHAPTER 4

# All the Right Moves

Understanding Windows' user interface goes beyond learning how to run pull-down menus. When we talk about hardware, "user interface" pertains to the mouse, keyboard, and monitor (the parts of the PC that interface with the you, the user). Making the best use of these components is the key to understanding — and *enjoying* — Windows. We'll tell you some interesting things about:

- Mice
- Keyboards
- Monitors
- Virtual screens

# OPTIMIZING YOUR SYSTEM

## ▶ Building a better mouse

> Every Windows user understands how to use a mouse. You can use mouse utilities to launch applications and automate many Windows activities.

The Windows mouse, as animals go, is pretty darn dumb. Point. Click. Drag. Sleep. And while there is some deviation, almost every mouse command uses a single button.

There is a way to teach that old mouse new tricks using utilities such as Whiskers, Right On, or Power Launcher. These utilities let you define functions for the right (or middle, if you have a three-button unit) mouse button. For instance, the right button could be used instead of the Enter key, while the middle button could trigger a File Save command.

There's more. Each of the three mouse buttons can be programmed in conjunction with the Ctrl, Alt, or Shift keys, to perform functions or even load applications. For instance, Alt-middle button could fire up Excel. Whiskers takes everything a step further, building an application launcher and a macro recorder into its menu. Right On (Figure 4-4) adds value by installing itself into a Control Box menu that's accessible from any application. Power Launcher is a collection of advanced utilities, of which mouse programming is only one.

**Figure 4-4**
The Right On! control panel allows programming three mouse buttons.

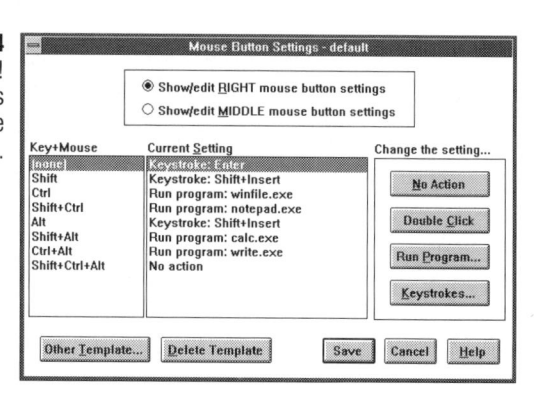

CHAPTER 4

## ▶ The key to success

> Although Windows is designed for use with mice, using the keyboard is frequently the faster option, particularly when running Windows on a laptop.

As Frank S. might say, Windows and the mouse go together like love and marriage. One without the other isn't quite the same. But there are times when a threesome is in order. While you can perform any Windows function with a mouse, there is (Solitaire notwithstanding) always a corresponding keyboard command. And sometimes it's the keyboard that provides the shortest distance between two points.

If you're in trouble with Windows, there are two keys that will almost always bail you out: Enter and Esc. If the machine freezes, chances are one or the other will jar things loose.

There is a method to the Enter key that provides generally universal command execution. When a dialogue box pops up with one or more options, the default — the option activated with the Enter key — will be highlighted by a border. This choice is usually "safe," one that causes minimal risk to the system and its files.

The Alt key is another universal key. Alt always takes you to the menu level. At that point, pressing the highlighted (underlined) letter will execute that command.

The Tab key is also extremely handy. It "jumps" you from one field to another in a dialog box.

Want to boost your speed and efficiency in five minutes or less? Sit down in front of your computer and execute the following 12 universal Windows keyboard commands. Do them five times each, so they start to feel natural:

## Shortcut Key Combinations

| Press this key combination | To accomplish this |
|---|---|
| Alt or F10 | Access menu bar |
| Alt-F4 | Close current application |
| Ctrl-Esc | Call up Task List |
| Alt-spacebar or Alt-hyphen | Call Control Box |
| Alt-spacebar+M or Alt-hyphen+M (or Alt-F10) | Maximize current window |
| Alt-spacebar+N or Alt-hyphen+N (or Alt-F9) | Minimize current window |
| Shift-F4 | Tile all active windows |
| Shift-F5 | Cascades all active windows |
| Ctrl-F6 | Moves to next active window |
| Alt-F-S | Saves active file |
| Alt-Tab | Next application |
| Shift-Alt-Tab | Last application |

Windows users who want to get full use out of the keyboard will be at a disadvantage on some machines. The standard PC keyboard positions its function keys across the top, although it's usually easier to execute function key commands if they are located on the left. For this reason, a third party keyboard from Northgate or Zeos will be a Windows timesaver. And this doesn't even take into account the improved touch and smooth key action.

## CHAPTER 4

▶ **Video games**

> EGA monitors are hardly worth it these days, either for the money or the quality. Get a color VGA or super VGA monitor.

Video hardware is the safest and most consistent part of assembling Windows. Part of the credit goes to the Video Graphics Array (VGA), the relatively high-resolution standard introduced by IBM in 1987. VGA is both inexpensive (you can add a card/monitor combination to a system for $350 or less) and superior: the 640 x 480 pixel resolution of the standard VGA screen gives Windows crispness and clarity.

By contrast, looking at Windows on an EGA system (an older standard with 640 x 350 pixel resolution) is like computing through cheesecloth.

Similarly, if you've been using VGA for a while, it may be time to take the next logical step. Many new PCs are equipped with the noticeably sharper Super VGA (1024 x 768 pixels). More compelling, however, is an increase in size. Fifteen-inch monitors — an inch bigger than the standard — are gaining popularity, but you'll notice a *real* improvement with a 17" Super VGA screen. Another alternative comes from larger gray scale monitors, although few self-respecting Windows users will sacrifice their color option voluntarily. In either case, a greater screen size allows you to have more Windows open at once.

By the way, there are monochrome VGA and Super VGA monitors for about a third the price of their color counterparts. If you've never used a color monitor of any kind before, you may be able to use a monochrome monitor and enjoy it. But it's sort of like watching a B&W TV after having watched a color TV for a while: you know that you're seeing the same show, but it's not as much fun. Unless you're really trying to save money, buy the best color VGA monitor you can afford.

## ▶ Virtual screens

> "Virtual screens," like "virtual memory," let you squeeze more out of your equipment by giving you several screens you can switch between.

One of the wonderful by-products of all this technology is the opportunity to learn fancy new words and revised definitions for the old ones. With regard to Windows, "virtual" pertains to multitasking. In enhanced mode, Windows creates a "virtual machine" for each DOS application, allocating it a full 640K of memory. This enviable trick is accomplished by fooling the applications into thinking that hard disk space is actually RAM. In theory, this gives you unlimited potential to run DOS applications and tempts users to use Windows simply as a task switching device.

There is no reason that such a nifty word can't be used more than once. With that in mind, we are now seeing a plethora of so-called "virtual screen" programs, which extend the viewable area of the Windows environment. Essentially, a virtual screen program turns your monitor into an adjustable peephole onto the desktop. You move this viewer around to expand the workspace, as if it were a magnifying glass over a large canvas.

The great news about these programs is the ability to create several independent desktops (hence the name). Each quadrant becomes an area unto itself, which can contain several programs and icons. So on Desktop #1, you can have Word for Windows and Grammatik, and dedicate file management to Desktop #2. Crosstalk can sit on Desktop #3, while a phonebook program occupies Desktop #4. Each space can also host minimized icons that pertain to the main application. The possibilities are endless, or at least virtual.

Generally, the more applications you use, the slower the machine will be. So "virtual" isn't always "better." On the other hand, if you have a RAM-robust PC and well-behaved applications, a virtual utility offers a better way to switch back and forth between programs than the standard Task List.

One virtual solution is a grid, like Baseline Publishing's Virtual Monitors or Attitash Software's Wide Angle 2.0. The problem with the original Wide Angle wasn't really Wide Angle's problem, it was the tendency of applications to hog system memory. The evolution in applications, along with some welcome improvements, places Wide Angle at the head of the pack (although Virtual Monitors allows you to use the keypad to switch between screens).

Wide Angle's icon is divided into eleven segments. Clicking on any of the numbers from 1 to 9 takes you to that desktop. System functions are modified through its Control Box, which is about one-sixth of the standard Windows component, while the icon's upper right-hand section calls up Wide Angle's "x-ray view." This value-added icon shows how the power of these little squares can be harnessed, although some detail-wary users might not perceive this as an advantage. The icon is always visible — you can move it to whatever corner of the screen is the least obtrusive — and a mouse click takes you to any of the either other desktops with deliberate speed.

Wide Angle has a number of welcome extras. You can designate each desktop for a specific function and automatically load grouped applications. Certain desktops can be assigned as DOS areas and run non-Windows applications in full-screen mode (where virtual meets virtual). And a desktop map view shows where all applications are at a particular time, and allow you to relocate them in whatever way you please.

Furthermore, the x-ray view acts as a smart task list, locating each application without regard to the nine virtual desktops. This is massively helpful, especially for people with messy desks. (Just because you are given more space, it doesn't mean that things will automatically become less disorganized.)

Another "virtual" option comes from Aristosoft's More-Windows. Instead of several adjoining compartmentalized screens, MoreWindows enlarges the desk space into a single entity. Here, the porthole analogy becomes more appropriate. You are given access to a larger screen, scrolling wide or deep to gain access to another corner of the document. The monitor becomes a magnifying glass.

This notion takes some getting used to. As you slide the mouse, it extends to another part of the spreadsheet or document in a rolling motion. Applications come up huge and need to be resized to fit the MoreWindows environment. Using this program can make you dizzy quickly.

At the same time, if you have a large and wide document or spreadsheet, MoreWindows offers fast and convenient access to data that may be a part of the periphery. You can use MoreWindows to view one giant document, or to allocate corners of the giant desktop to different programs. For instance, you can (once you've mastered the fine points of scrolling mouse motion) be using Word for Windows and then just slide on over to Crosstalk to check your MCI mailbox.

A third type of virtual thinking comes from Xerox's new Room for Windows. This takes the whole concept a few steps further, allowing you to install different wallpaper schemes in each virtual "room." Here, you can have as many — or as few — rooms as memory and resources allow, and the program is a lot more customizable than either of the alternatives.

While there are several standalone "virtual" options from which to choose, virtual screens have become part of several Windows utilities packages. Among these, hDC's Power Launcher and Tools Technologies' Big Sky allow you to designate the number of screens to install, instead of an arbitrary number. Consequently, once this ability becomes part of every utility, virtual screens could become the Icon Designer of Windows 3.1: everyone will have one, so the capability will be almost entirely generic. In any case, getting virtual can expand your options and turn task switching into less of a task.

CHAPTER 4

# Summing Up

Fine-tuning the Windows system is one of the least "fun" aspects of Windows ownership. For pure enjoyment it doesn't compare with some of the tips contained in other chapters. On the other hand, an efficient user is a happy user. If you end up getting your fingernails dirty messing around with a CONFIG.SYS file, the increase in speed and power will be worth the price of a new manicure.

Using Windows isn't as transparent as we'd all like. On the other hand, it doesn't take that much effort to master or refine the system, both on a hardware or software level. And tweaking it is just a matter of practice.

# 5

## custom made

# Windows

**Tweaking your system for maximum convenience and delight**

Once the system's hardware and software is stable, there follows a never-ending upgrade. Too often we use car analogies to describe computers, but a Windows-driven PC may be more like a boat. The boat comparison holds more water, because Windows users may use it part-time to get from one point to another, or they may actually live full-time in the environment.

There are limits to what a Windows PC can do. You still can't sail around the world. But there are plenty of things you can add to make your environment more comfortable and appealing.

In this chapter, we'll teach you to have it your way by:

- Customizing WIN.INI in a variety of ways
- Changing your Windows startup screen and the wallpaper
- Using DOS shells other than Program Manager
- Tweaking your screen colors
- Modifying and creating icons

CHAPTER 5

# WIN.INI is Everything

Initialization — or INI — files are an important part of Windows. They contain short programmer-ese statements that determine various system and software settings. At setup or the first time you run them, many programs create their own separate .INI files that govern how those programs work.

The mother of all these files is WIN.INI (see Figure 5-1), which holds startup information about both the Windows system and individual applications. Closely related is SYSTEM.INI, which contains settings for the computer as a whole, such as the video display and the network driver. Like the AUTOEXEC.BAT and CONFIG.SYS files from the DOS world, you can go through life ignoring WIN.INI. Modifications will be made automatically for you by various programs.

**Figure 5-1**
The WIN.INI file categorizes system settings under different headings.

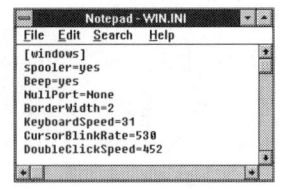

```
Notepad - WIN.INI
File  Edit  Search  Help
[windows]
spooler=yes
Beep=yes
NullPort=None
BorderWidth=2
KeyboardSpeed=31
CursorBlinkRate=530
DoubleClickSpeed=452
```

But if you prefer, you can take an aggressive part in WIN.INI revision. This will result in a more finely tuned Windows engine. Because of Windows' amazing flexibility, you can even turn your system into the PC equivalent of a custom hot-rod. It all depends on how much time you want to spend under the hood. (See, you didn't have to wait too long for a car analogy after all.)

This section will explain how to:

- Maneuver through the jungles of WIN.INI
- Keep WIN.INI trimmed down to size
- Install SYSEDIT.EXE, a better editor than Notepad

## Mini Review — The Norton Desktop for Windows

Although Norton Desktop for Windows (see Figure 5-2) provides a great replacement for ProgMan, it also comes with many useful utilities, such as undelete, system information, and disk maintenance. It was also the first program to make "drag and drop" technology work in an instinctive way. The program is also chock-full of customizing touches, such as the ability to install desktop buttons linked to applications and files. One mouseclick can check MCI Mail or load a spreadsheet. When the project's finished, you can easily make the button disappear.

**Figure 5-2**
The Norton Desktop for Windows provides an abundance of information and controls.

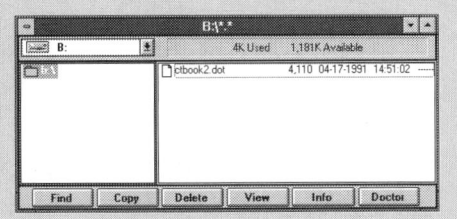

One drawback: you need to expend a lot of energy to receive NDW's benefits. It's visual aspects are similar to Windows 3.1, so buying Norton may in some ways seem redundant (although 3.1 doesn't have nearly the breadth of utilities that Norton contains). In addition, the system enhancements brought forth by NDW exceed the power and pizazz of many applications, giving the Windows user that too-familiar all-dressed-up-with-no-place-to-go feeling.

## ▶ Navigating WIN.INI

> WIN.INI contains controls and information for Windows and the Windows applications you've installed under bracketed headings like [Windows Help]

Initially, WIN.INI contains controls for the system and for some of the applets (Notepad, Terminal, and so on) that come with Windows. When you install a new program, the installation process often adds a new section to WIN.INI devoted to that program.

But what if you want to delete that program? Or see for yourself what its settings are? Or manually edit settings? In those cases, you'll need to be able to find your way around.

It's not hard. WIN.INI is divided into sections, which are signalled by names inside square brackets. For instance, the [desktop] section controls what the desktop looks like.

So far, so good. Underneath each section name you'll find settings. They follow the syntax name of *setting = value*. Thus, the setting Spooler=Yes tells Windows to use the Print Manager for spooling print files. Spooler=No would disable Print Manager.

Later in this chapter, we'll show you how to modify WIN.INI indirectly with Control Panel or directly with a text editor.

### Inside WIN.INI

| What It Is | What it Does |
| --- | --- |
| [windows] | Governs overall elements in the Windows environment such as the application loaded when Windows starts, the mouse speed and button configuration, and keyboard speed |
| [Desktop] | Controls the appearance of the screen background and icon positioning |

## CUSTOM MADE WINDOWS

| What It Is | What it Does |
|---|---|
| [Extensions] | Associates file types (suffixes) with applications so double-checking on the file name will automatically load the application |
| [intl] | Controls settings for countries outside of the US |
| [ports] | Lists all available output ports |
| [fonts] | Describes all installed screen font files |
| [Windows Help] | Controls the settings for Windows Help |
| [*printer ports*] | Lists specific information for each of the available output devices |
| [*devices*] | Lists active output devices compatible with Windows 2.x applications |
| [colors] | Lists the numerical value of all colors used in the Windows display |
| [*program name*] | Lists startup settings and special-conditions for a specific Windows application |

*Warning* Before modifying any INI file, you should back it up. A good procedure is to give the copy an extension that corresponds with the date — such SYSTEM.818.

## ▶ The WIN.INI skinny

Keep WIN.INI lean and mean by deleting unneeded sections.

WIN.INI can grow to huge proportions, so an active Windows pioneer should regularly examine the WIN.INI file and delete any unnecessary references. For instance, almost every Windows application leaves some kind of mark in the WIN.INI. These little references mount up. If you delete an application, don't forget to cut the corresponding WIN.INI notations.

Microsoft recommends that you keep WIN.INI to around 54K. Larger files may run without problem. Or they may not. Or they may cause sporadic problems and excessive loading times. If your system's acting weird for no apparent reason, you may need to trim the fat from WIN.INI. You can do so with Notepad, SysEdit, or any other text editor.

## ▶ The fast way to get into .INIs

> The easiest way to edit WIN.INI and SYSTEM.INI is with SysEdit, but you must first install SysEdit in a program group.

At setup, Windows installs a handful of utilities that help to fine-tune the environment, such as Notepad. But the useful System Editor, called SysEdit, needs to be installed manually. SysEdit is an undocumented but popular editor included with Windows 3.0 and 3.1.

SysEdit has one function — the editing of important system files. When you launch SysEdit, it immediately opens four Windows containing four key files (Figure 5-3):

**Figure 5-3**
System Edit is a four-headed utility dedicated solely to editing system files.

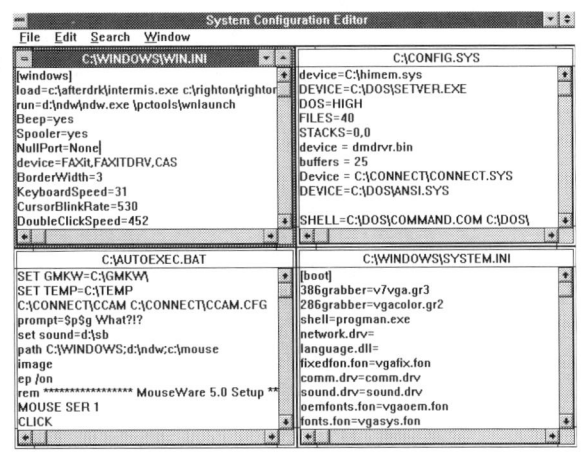

To install SysEdit, do the following:

1. Switch to the Main group in the Program Manager.
2. Select File New.
3. Select New/Program Item.
4. Type \windows\system\sysedit.exe in the command-line box.
5. Save and exit.

Once you've followed these steps, the SysEdit icon will appear in the main program group. You now have the key to more efficient system maintenance.

CHAPTER 5

# Dress for Success

As you've seen, Windows runs just fine right out of the box. But to use the car analogy again, you may want to give it a custom paint job. Sure, it still runs the same, but it looks so much snazzier with a candy-apple red finish and a clean dashboard.

In this section, we'll show you how to:

- Remove the Microsoft Windows logo...
- ...and replace it with one of your own
- Adjust the distance between icons
- Speed up Windows by removing your wallpaper

## ▶ No word from our sponsor

> The logo you see when you start Windows may lose some of its appeal after the first few hundred times. Start Windows by typing **WIN :** to skip the logo.

The first thing you see after starting up Windows is a big, blue (!) Microsoft logo that holds the screen for a few seconds before loading the program. For those who want to escape such subliminal seduction, there are a few ways to make your computer more like public TV. When you start Windows, add a space and a colon to the WIN command, like this:

```
WIN :
```

When you start Windows like this, the screen will be black for the moment when it would have shown the Microsoft Windows logo.

## ▶ A word from *your* sponsor

> Having removed Microsoft's startup logo, you can use WINGIF to add your own custom logo.

The logical next step after ridding yourself of Microsoft's unwanted plug is to substitute it with one of your own. This operation takes a few steps and — unless you are a programmer or get all your software for free — some money. Whether or not it's too stiff a price to pay to escape a forced few seconds with Microsoft's logo is left as a bonus exercise for the reader.

The three steps to a commercial free environment are:

**Selection.** If you've decided that the Microsoft logo is the wrong way to start the day, you'll need to select something more appropriate. Theoretically, you can use any bitmapped image, be it Bart Simpson or the Sistine Chapel (subject to copyright laws, of course).

**Conversion.** In order to be displayed at startup, a bitmap must be converted to RLE file format. This is simple enough if you have a conversion program such as the shareware WINGIF. Load the selected bitmap into the conversion program as a 4-bit-per-pixel RLE file. Save and attach an RLE suffix.

**Installation.** Once you've created the file (let's call it BART.RLE) you need to reconfigure the WIN.COM file to allow for the new image. To accomplish this, you need to exit Windows and work with the DOS prompt.

1. Copy BART.RLE to the \windows\system\ directory. Make sure the files WIN.CNF and VGALOGO.LGO are also in that directory.

2. Type the following:
   ```
   copy /b win.cnf+vgalgo.lgo+c\bart.rle win2.com
   ```

"Win2" is arbitrary. It will serve as your new startup command so it can be anything from "mom" to "apple-pie." When you start Windows with this command, Bart's

## CUSTOM MADE WINDOWS

visage will grace your screen instead of the once-offensive Microsoft logo.

This is a diverting trick that makes your Windows system more customizable. Still, it's best suited to people with a lot of time on their hands and a burning desire to express their individuality.

CHAPTER 5

> ### Elbow room
>
> Icons with long names may overlap when they're minimized at the bottom of the screen. Adjusting the icon spacing will let you read everything clearly.

When minimized, icons are lined up across the bottom of the desktop. Each program, however, attaches a label of varying length that may contain the program name, file name, and pathname — all adding up to a serious case of the visual run-ons.

The solution comes from the Desktop module of the Control Panel, with a numerical Icon Spacing Command. Adjusted to 125 to 150 pixels, this should allow enough room for icons to co-exist.

## CUSTOM MADE WINDOWS

### ▶ Useless Windows dressing

> Wallpaper uses up bunches of system resources you may not have to spare. Running without it will speed up load time and give Windows that much more room.

Windows wallpaper, which covers the desktop with a bitmapped image, is a good illustration of Windows' graphical ability, how any drawing, photograph or artwork, can be displayed with clarity on a VGA screen. Once the demonstration is finished, however, this module has little use. In fact, using wallpaper can be detrimental to your computing health — it uses RAM, system resources, and hard disk space, with no increase in productivity.

To be sure, "increasing productivity" is not what Windows is about, as it's intended to bring a sense of fun to personal computing. There is nothing wrong with visual frivolity, but the resources that wallpaper saps — memory, resources and storage — are not infinite. Popping up a picture of Elvis or Mom will hardly be worth the slowdown, and why anyone would want to stare at chess pieces or zigzags for any length of time is beyond comprehension (Figure 5-4).

**Figure 5-4**
Windows' bitmap ZIGS.BMP can be used as wallpaper. Who cares?

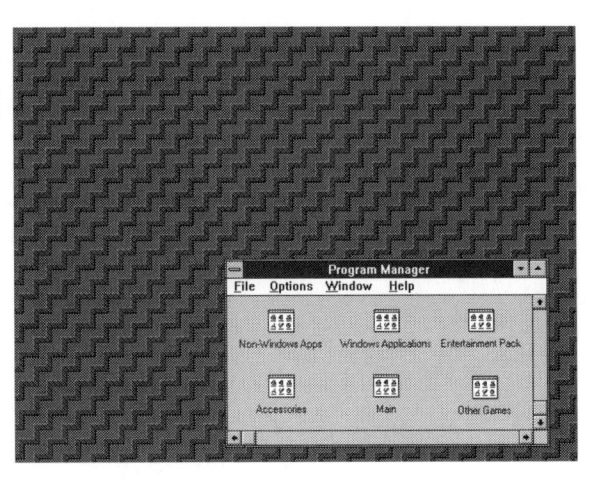

You still want to use wallpaper? Some people never learn. But even if there is no way to save memory and system resources, you can at least minimize the storage drain by

## CHAPTER 5

compressing bitmap files into .RLE format. This is accomplished with WINGIF or another graphics conversion package. The compressed file can be installed in the desktop wallpaper module and called from this format.

# Gimme Shell-ter

The DOS shell concept, where common system commands are organized in a comprehensible way, has both similarities and differences with regard to Windows. Similarly, a diversity of shells are available for Windows, from rudimentary images to those that look like the control panel of a 747. Unlike DOS, however, a shell is required for Windows operation. You can't run Windows without a shell, any more than you can drive a car without a dashboard.

The default shell is Program Manager, dubbed ProgMan. ProgMan isn't bad — it manages icons and programs competently — but it will be too much for some users and not enough for others.

In this section, we'll explore the following:

- Changing the Windows shell from ProgMan to any of several alternatives (one of which is free)

- Improving the Task Manager or replacing it with a third-party product

## ▶ Which shell is Windows under?

> You're not stuck with ProgMan; you can use any Windows program as the shell.

To change the shell, open up SYSTEM.INI and write the name of the new shell (suffix included) on the Shell= line. The change will take effect when you restart.

Any Window program can function as a shell. Functionally, the shell becomes the last program loaded, full-screen, at start up. If you choose Word for Windows as a shell, Windows will open into that program. Practically, however, a shell needs to have the capacity to run other applications from its menus. This can be as simple as containing a "run" command in its control box, or as complicated as a full-blown program and icon management facility. For instance, with Word for Windows loaded as a shell, a user will be able to do nothing with the system aside from word processing. This is one way an employer can control how a company's PCs are used and keep people from playing Solitaire.

Replacement shells vary in size, power, and functions. Here are three examples of shells, that use, respectively, light, medium, and heavy approaches to the concept. Similarly, each of the three also requires increased memory and system resources.

### The light approach
When designing a Windows desktop and workspace, there are ways to go light and lean. The first step is to install a skinny utility as a shell. Two options are Launch, a shareware program that's basically a single menu, or the substitute Task Manager in Metz Software's File F/X utilities package (Figure 5-5). Both options are unpretentious and unspectacular, but they place all common commands in easy reach. This solution is for relatively savvy users who know their way around Windows, or who can solve problems without relying on Program Manager.

**Figure 5-5**
Metz Software's Task Manager is a low-calorie shell.

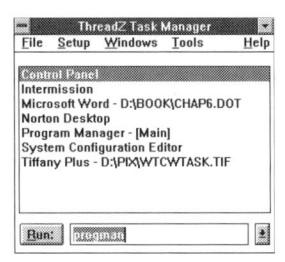

An added touch for this slimmed-down option is to add hDC's Microapps and Power Launcher, which installs into the Control Box of every window and provides several essential system and file management functions.

### The middle ground

Although it was once Windows' face to the world, MS-DOS Executive was unceremoniously dumped when Windows 3.0 came along. Users, Microsoft felt, wanted something more explicit than a half-graphical text list. For many users, MS-DOS Exec is forgotten, but not gone. While Setup does not install it in the main group, it's alive and well in your Windows subdirectory (Figure 5-6).

Oddly enough, the same people who complained about Exec's clunkiness now appreciate its style. Its abilities fall somewhere between the DOS prompt and Program Manager. It will probably be most appreciated by people who understand DOS commands and hate shells that are too touchie-feelie. So MS-DOS' bare bones style, a failure as a main interface, finds a home as a file management tool. In fact, it's one of the fastest ways to accomplish a simple file copy or delete from within Windows.

As a shell, MS-DOS Exec will be best for people who know both DOS and Windows, and don't need everything spelled out. By using Exec as a desktop and loading standard applications in the WIN.INI file, you'll end up with a relatively lean, productive desktop.

## CHAPTER 5

**Figure 5-6**
The once-outdated MS-DOS Executive is a good way for DOS-wise users to manage files.

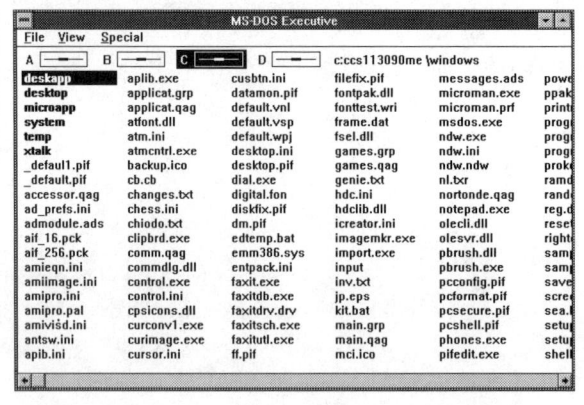

| \_ | MS-DOS Executive | ▼ ▲ |
|---|---|---|
| File View Special | | |

```
A ═══  B ═══  C ═══  D ═══   c:ccs113090me \windows
deskapp       aplib.exe     cusbtn.ini     filefix.pif    messages.ads   pow
desktop       applicat.grp  datamon.pif    fontpak.dll    microman.exe   ppak
microapp      applicat.qag  default.vnl    fonttest.wri   microman.prf   print
system        atfont.dll    default.vsp    frame.dat      msdos.exe      prog
temp          atm.ini       default.wpj    fsel.dll       ndw.exe        prog
xtalk         atmcntrl.exe  desktop.ini    games.grp      ndw.ini        prog
_defaul1.pif  backup.ico    desktop.pif    games.qag      ndw.ndw        prok
_default.pif  cb.cb         dial.exe       genie.txt      nl.txr         ramd
accessor.qag  changes.txt   digital.fon    hdc.ini        nortonde.qag   rand
ad_prefs.ini  chess.ini     diskfix.pif    hdclib.dll     notepad.exe    reg.d
admodule.ads  chiodo.txt    dm.pif         icreator.ini   olecli.dll     rese
aif_16.pck    clipbrd.exe   edtemp.bat     imagemkr.exe   olesvr.dll     right
aif_256.pck   comm.qag      emm386.sys     import.exe     pbrush.dll     samp
amieqn.ini    commdlg.dll   entpack.ini    input          pbrush.exe     samp
amiimage.ini  control.exe   faxit.exe      inv.txt        pcconfig.pif   save
amipro.ini    control.ini   faxitdb.exe    jp.eps         pcformat.pif   scre
amipro.pal    cpsicons.dll  faxitdrv.drv   kit.bat        pcsecure.pif   sea.b
amivisd.ini   curconv1.exe  faxitsch.exe   main.grp       pcshell.pif    setu
antsw.ini     curimage.exe  faxitutl.exe   main.qag       phones.exe     setu
apib.ini      cursor.ini    ff.pif         mci.ico        pifedit.exe    shell
```

Some people will want a Big Desktop, something with the power to command and control all system functions. This path will be followed by people who have substantial tasks to complete and system resources to spare, and can go one of two ways: either graphical, where icons and images prevail, or traditional, with the standard file/list interface serving as the shell.

A graphical option, like Aporia or PubTech File Organizer, seeks to make Windows like the Mac, installing drag-and-drop icons and an increased reliance on icon-driven commands. These programs make things easier — eventually. Consistency is still elusive and different shells have different philosophies. This is a subjective judgement, as one person's intuitive program will be another's dBASE IV.

### A really heavy number

File-oriented shells are best for users who know DOS and can easily manage files and trees. A successful Windows shell in this category will add graphical aspects to the file/tree structure. A good example is Becker Tools (Figure 5-7), which features two file windows and a multitude of small icons. At first glance, Becker appears cluttered and confusing; in fact, the icon covered by the cursor is explained on the status line. With this type of safety net, it becomes easy to learn what icon controls which function, even if the images are a little obscure.

**CUSTOM MADE WINDOWS**

**Figure 5-7**
The Becker Tools interface is more complicated than small aircraft control panels.

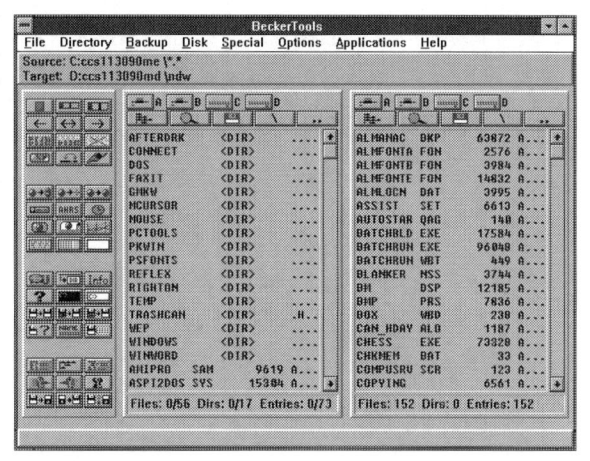

A "heavy" shell — of which ProgMan is almost one — takes a lot of time to learn and resources to run. The payback is that the right shell will manage your files and your system comprehensively, so you don't need to switch back and forth to PC Tools every time there's a job to be done.

## ➤ Enhancing task manager

> The Task Manager is not as useful as it once was. There are many good alternatives on the market.

Task Manager is a useful Windows utility. It lists all open applications and promotes fast task switching. This handy little list is accessible two ways — through a Ctrl-Esc keystroke or by double clicking on the desktop.

There are a couple of ways to enhance Task Manager. One is to replace it with a similar (but more powerful) utility. One such comes from Metz Software. This enhanced utility features an application launcher, screen saver interface, and run command, essentially borrowing and reallocating some often-used Program Manager controls.

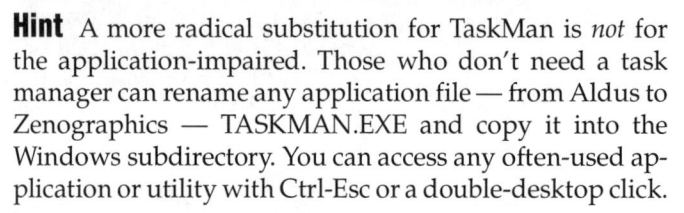

➤ **Hint** A more radical substitution for TaskMan is *not* for the application-impaired. Those who don't need a task manager can rename any application file — from Aldus to Zenographics — TASKMAN.EXE and copy it into the Windows subdirectory. You can access any often-used application or utility with Ctrl-Esc or a double-desktop click.

Task Manager itself is, in fact, becoming less important as an increasing amount of applications install TaskMan substitutes. Norton Desktop for Windows, for one, inserts an optional Task List item on the Control Box menu so you can access any open application from within any other. So does hDC's Power Launcher. DeskTopSet, a multi-module time management utility, has a pair of index cards on each menu that similarly lists all open applications. And AmiPro 2.0 comes with a pre-packaged macro that installs a task manager choice on the menu. With any of these, another open application is but a mouse-click away.

# Hue and Cry

The first thing you notice about Windows is the variety of cool colors available for your use. Or maybe it isn't. In fact, the pre-configured color schemes provided with Windows are, despite some fairly intriguing names, pretty darn boring. For one thing, all of them use white as the default window color. While this has its place (as we'll discuss later), when it comes to colors the new Windows user is like a kid in a candy store. And you don't want to be stuck with nothing but licorice.

Messing around with the color selection module, which is part of the control panel, is probably the best way to get acquainted with the Windows interface. Designing a new color scheme is as easy as buying one off the rack. All you do is mouse click on the area to be modified, then select a color from the palette. A representation of the color scheme is displayed, but you can't really tell how it will look until the scheme is loaded full-screen. The things you'll learn here are:

- What the color selection module is, and how to use it
- How to save different color patterns to suit your every whimsical mood
- How *not* to overdo it
- How to set up screen colors for those times when you're doing screen shots of Windows applications

CHAPTER 5

## ▶ Learn your way around

*The color selection module in the Control Panel is probably the easiest part of Windows to use.*

The Windows color selection module in the Control Panel should be one of the first Windows programs you try. Not only does it help to shape your environment, it makes it easy to learn the different parts of the interface — answering those age old queries "What's a desktop?" and "How do you differentiate an active and inactive window?"

The color selection module spells it out for you in an easy to understand way. You start Control Panel and select Color (Figure 5-8). In the dialog box, you point at any of the screen elements (which are labeled near the top of the dialog box), then select the color to be used for that part. Extra help comes from a drop-down list box, which reiterates the segment under modification.

**Figure 5-8**
Windows' color control takes you into the shade.

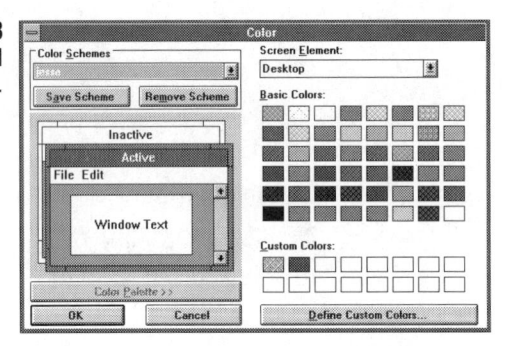

This layout makes the parts of the Windows interface remarkably easy to learn. For instance, you may have associated red as an active hue because of your bullfighting days and yellow as inactive because it was the color of slug-like Uncle Oswald's tie. You'd then color the active and inactive windows accordingly.

## ▶ Dare to be diverse

After years being stuck with boring CGA and EGA colors, you can choose rich, vibrant shades and hues. Go for the gusto!

The worst part about changing colors on many DOS programs — aside from the general blandness of the available shades — is the difficulty of the process. Windows not only allows a quick change, you can also create and load an infinite amount of color schemes to be switched back and forth at will. After creating a desirable scheme (some layouts, to be honest, won't be worth saving) click the "Save Scheme" button and assign a name. The pattern is then saved for posterity.

The potential here is to have several color schemes that reflect different moods or projects. This flexibility adds flash to the system and will be utilized by the same type of person who wore psychedelic pants in eighth grade.

## CHAPTER 5

### ▶ Dare to be productive

> You need to choose your colors with some care. Hot pink letters on an emerald background will not encourage productivity and may, in fact, result in an irresistible urge to return to the sixties.

There aren't a lot of things you can do with the Windows color module and still expect to get some work done. First of all, there are only two types of people in the world: those who like dark text on a light background, and those who prefer otherwise. You need to select a clear, readable shade for your main window, along with an appropriately opposite hue for text. You repeat the process for every other facet — menus, borders, and scroll bars. Whatever color you choose needs to provide contrast to the surrounding shades (Figure 5-9).

**Figure 5-9**
Windows' color module lets you mix your own color creation of custom dithered colors.

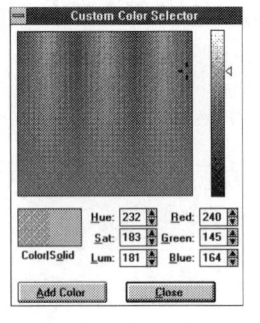

Windows' colors are of two types: *dithered* and pure. The easy way to tell them apart is that dithered seems to show a texture or weave. Dithered colors, also, cannot be used as background shades for the main window or menu bar. This may decrease flexibility somewhat, but correspondingly decreases eye strain.

As for pure colors, Windows itself recognizes only 16 at a time. This limitation isn't really limiting due to the ability to dither and the fact that an effective color scheme doesn't need more than five or six shades. The trick, however, is finding those five or six that make you feel comfortable. If it's a slightly tricky trial-and-error operation, it's still a lot easier than shopping for carpet.

Still, we can give you a few pointers that will make you more productive:

- Keeping the active window and text very bright and easy to see prevents clicking on the wrong window and prevents errors in ProgMan and FileMan

- As long as you don't have problems with screen flicker (see below), you should use white for the workspace for the truest WYSIWYG (What You See Is What You Get) representation of the final printed page

- If you do have a screen that flickers, try a light gray workspace instead of white, or experiment with white text on black background

- Colored buttons are probably more noticeable

Finally, when you're setting up your screen colors, remember basic color psychology principles. Use "hot" colors like reds and oranges for warnings or things you want to notice quickly. "Cooler" colors such as blues and greens are easier to look at for long periods of time.

## Dare to be dull

> Fancy colors are not always the thing you need. If you're doing screen captures of Windows applications, use undithered colors or monochrome.

Computer books, magazines and posters show users what should be on their screen to effectively complete a certain task — a case of WYSOTPIWYS-GOYIM (What You See On This Page Is What You Should Get On Your Individual Monitor).

The art of creating stunning screen shots is a gentle one, governed by a few simple rules. First of all, dithered colors look like ground gruel when they're transferred to the black and white of a printed page. A truly generic color scheme — one that relies on grays and whites — will be the best choice for those who need to create screen representations for reproduction in a monochrome environment. To achieve this true neutrality, set the following in the "colors" section of the WIN.INI file:

```
Background=192 192 192
AppWorkspace=0 255 232
Window=255 255 255
WindowText=0 0 0
Menu=255 255 255
MenuText=0 0 0
ActiveTitle=0 0 128
InactiveTitle=255 255 255
TitleText=255 255 255
ActiveBorder=128 128 128
InactiveBorder=255 255 255
WindowFrame=0 0 0
Scrollbar=192 192 192
```

This may border on Dullsville, but sometimes an explicit line drawing better communicates the message than a fancy abstract painting.

# Icon Get No Satisfaction

An essential part of the Windows interface is the *icon*, a visual representation of files and applications. This little drawing has a big responsibility. It's supposed to tell you what the linked program does, or otherwise give some indication as to the content of the linked file.

Icon development and design has become a cottage industry, one of the busiest Windows aftermarkets. Today's products have the characteristics of a paint program with arcs, fills, shading, and all kinds of details.

On the surface, spending time on icons may seem frivolous — and, indeed, it can be. On the other hand, if substituting icons makes it easier to find what you want in a crowded group window, then you've boosted productivity. (Keep telling yourself how much more productive you're becoming when you spend several hours creating icons; it'll do your heart good.)

In particular, those who use DOS programs will find it helpful to substitute meaningful icons for the bland, generic DOS icon provided by Windows.

Here are some keen ways to light up your icon life:

- Buy an icon library
- Build your own icons

CHAPTER 5

▶ **Get thee to a library**

Several packages of icons are commercially available. Substituting one icon for an existing icon is easy and fun.

Any icon modification package worth its salt includes a healthy image library. Icon Pak (Figure 5-10), in two volumes, was one of the first out of the gate. Although it proffered some interesting drawings, the price ($49 and $99) seemed a little steep for what you were getting — especially if you subscribe to the old-fashioned notion that software should actually do something.

**Figure 5-10**
An icon library file will have several images, often grouped by subject.

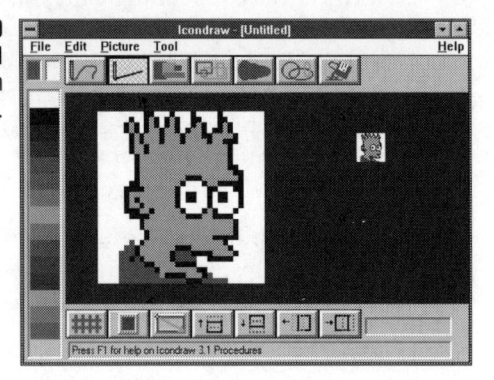

At any rate, substituting an icon in Program Manager applications groups is a relatively easy process:

1. Highlight the application.

2. Select File Properties in Program Manager.

3. Select Change Icon.

4. Type the name of the file that has the icon you want to use. Icon libraries have several images in one file, so you may have to click through to find the right one. PROGMAN.EXE comes with a wide selection of icons (Figure 5-11).

**Figure 5-11**
You can scroll through the range of icons in a library or program.

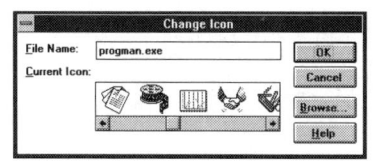

5. Click OK. This will return you to the Properties box, where you can type in a filename and an application name together. An icon can automatically load a file and perform a function. This works better with some applications than others. Those that don't allow more than one version of a program to run simultaneously may cause some problems.

CHAPTER 5

> **Build your own**
>
> Creating your own icon from scratch or customizing an existing icon is creative and interesting, even if your efforts may not be widely appreciated.

Icon design packages, as we mentioned, match the sophistication of many paint programs. Through careful pixel manipulation you can create a miniature masterpiece. That is, if you have a lot of time and talent to waste. You could spend a few hours working on a masterpiece that will eventually be relegated to the corner of a computer screen. At least the miniature paintings you buy on the boardwalk can be hung on the wall for the whole family to enjoy.

Perhaps the best way for the non-artistic user to develop a custom icon is to modify an existing image. Design tools will usually let you import a program's icon, then add your own touches. You can start by just changing the background color, then go wild.

Icon design, in any case, is a debatable art. You can spend hours developing the coolest icons known to humankind, yet very few people will see them or even know they exist. For those who have a dozen novels in the drawer and like to hide their artistic endeavor, icon design is the perfect way to fill your day. For everyone else, it's basically a waste of time. But who said you shouldn't waste a little time now and then?

Like any art subcategory, the icon market is changing quickly. Nevertheless, certain minimum standards have emerged. A decent icon design program will have:

- The ability to change executable files
- A selection of drawing and shading tools
- A view window so you can see a scale representation of the icon as it develops
- A library of at least 100 icons you can use as a jumping-off point
- At least one view of Bullwinkle J. Moose

## Summing Up

Polishing Windows is almost a full-time job. There are many ways to modify the environment on a day-to-day basis, and you're never finished. There are always little tweaks that make the environment a little prettier, along with ways to reflect a change in procedure, mood, or political orientation.

A lot of these visual adjustments mean nothing, and their value can't be quantified by bottom-line productivity gains. They can, however, keep you from getting bored, or make you feel a little better about spending half your life in front of a glowing screen.

# CHAPTER 5

# 6 — Fun & Functional

**A miscellany of utilities and tricks**

Once the Windows boat is seaworthy — the engine running and the sails in place — you'll embark on a new voyage across the PC seas. Like a boat, however, there's no end to the possible improvements or refinements of the Windows vessel. You may discover, after a while, that these individual refinements have little to do with reaching your destination, or, in computer parlance, Getting the Job Done. Rather, they are more along the lines of (to return to the boat analogy) fluffing a pillow on the lower deck or making sure that the port-a-fridge has enough garlic-stuffed olives for the entire voyage.

Which is not to say that the following tips — or any other second-level Windows modifications — are useless or stupid. With these, Windows demonstrates its ability to evolve with you; to accommodate the growth in your knowledge and needs with a corresponding expansion in power and capability.

CHAPTER 6

# Baby Steps

Windows comes right out of the box with several "applets" — little applications that demonstrate what Windows can do, such as Calculator, Write, and Terminal. Applets have just enough ability to do a simple task, but that's about it. For example, you wouldn't use Windows Write for any detailed textual exploration; you'd get a "serious" word processor. Similarly, other less noticeable modules benefit from improvement. If those who seek to enhance Notepad and Clipboard are "over the edge" when it comes to Windows fanaticism, you'll be able to tell them apart from the rest of the folks at the Windows regatta: their boat has all of the olives.

This section tells some of the things you can do with the applets, shows you alternatives to consider when you hit their limits, and discusses a few related topics, including:

- Adding ASCII editors to replace Notepad and SysEdit
- Using Scrapbook+ instead of Clipboard
- Installing hDC's DeskTopSet
- Recording macros with ProKey for Windows
- Replacing Clock with a Windows alarm clock
- Using a Windows or a DOS communications package instead of Terminal
- Learning more about telecommunications
- Installing a fax in your computer

## ▶ Who could ASCII for anything more?

Notepad and SysEdit are nothing to write home about, or with. WinEdit is a hot little ASCII editor for Windows.

Every Windows file has unique aspects that allow it to display visuals specific to the application with which it was created. System files and e-mail, however, don't take kindly to all the fancy formatting. You need pure, unadulterated ASCII files to get the message across.

Windows includes two ASCII-based tools, Notepad and SysEdit, for times when you want to keep the message pure. These applets are helpful, but their command structure is abbreviated and files are limited to 50,000 characters. Anyone doing a lot of work in ASCII may want to consider an enhanced Windows-based text editor.

Several such programs—with enhanced word wrap, windowing, or search abilities — are available as shareware. The BMW of text editors is the $59.95 WinEdit from Wilson WindowWare (Figure 6-1), which attaches a series of icon buttons to the top of every window. Half of these have to do with text manipulation, the rest are programming tools.

**Figure 6-1**
With its pushbutton icons, WinEdit is the BMW of Windows ASCII editors.

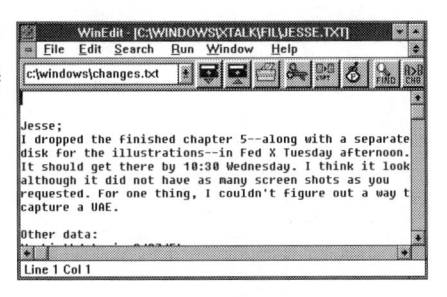

In the early days of computing, WinEdit would have been called a word processor — except no one would have thought to make the commands so clear and accessible. Even today, WinEdit has a few aspects that many other word processors could use, like the icon buttons and the ability to call up the past few files. Anybody who needs a program between Notepad and Word for Windows for text management will find WinEdit worthwhile.

## CHAPTER 6

### ▶ Scrappy contender

> Scrapbook+, a Clipboard substitute, saves multiple screen cuts and lets you store, retrieve, filter, and capture graphics.

The Windows Clipboard is an essential under-the-hood system module. While you may never need to select the Clipboard icon — and may in fact remove it to save system resources — you'll use the Clipboard every day. In simplest terms, when you cut anything from an application, it's stored in the Clipboard, where a paste command moves that data to any other place in the system. Unfortunately, the data stays in the Clipboard only until you make a new cut or copy. Copying several pieces of information from one application to another can involve several trips back and forth between apps.

One solution to this problem is to use a utility called Scrapbook+ (Figure 6-2). Not only does Scrapbook+ let you recall the last several Clipboard cuts, it also lets you store, retrieve, and filter graphic images and bit-maps. Scrapbook+ can even do screen captures, so you can "photograph" any image within Windows for import into Scrapbook+.

**Figure 6-2**
Scrapbook+ increases Clipboard power by storing images.

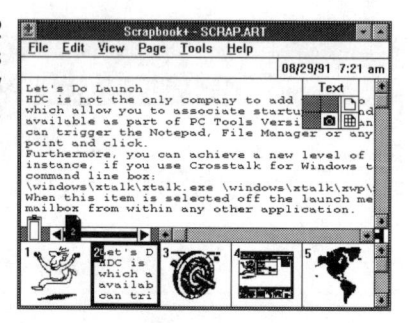

## FUN AND FUNCTIONAL

### ▶ The DeskTopSet

> DeskTopSet from hDC gives you a useful set of integrated desktop applets to replace Clock, Calendar, and Calculator.

You'd be hard pressed to find any real value in Windows' resident Clock, Calendar, and Calculator applets. There is little to recommend them in favor of their real-world counterparts. While hDC includes a neat little clock as part of its original MicroApps, Calendar and Calculator improvements come courtesy of Okna's versatile DeskTopSet (Figure 6-3).

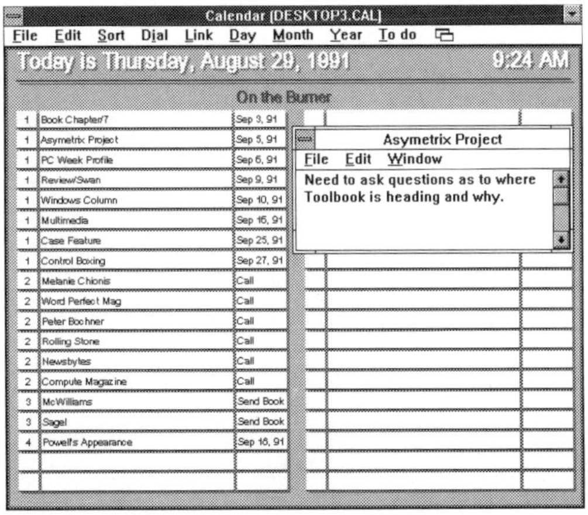

**Figure 6-3**
DeskTopSet allows you to make lists and tie notes to each item.

DeskTopSet is a calendar, calculator, phone book, and dialer that you can use together or separately. This modular integration (a necessary part of any successful Windows integrated package) lets you use what you want and ignore the rest. DeskTopSet's interface is also superior: the crisp and detailed screens recall the best of Asymetrix's ToolBook. The tape-styled calculator lets you keep a running numerical record, while the calendar allows several different views of a schedule. And, like the best Windows packages, you can attach a note to any field.

DeskTopSet's phonebook/dialer/log combination is a path to effective phone management using your PC, while the note facility lets you annotate personal references and conversations. You can also tie a separate phone list to each entry, adding a dimension that is certainly missing on a desktop phone directory.

The program's only real drawback is its tendency to usurp more than its share of system resources, making it impractical to leave these essential programs open all the time. This, unfortunately, limits their convenience.

## ▶ The cure for macrophobia

ProKey, a long-time DOS favorite, is now available for Windows. With ProKey you can create macros to automate Windows procedures.

The dirty word M-A-C-R-O ends up scaring away PC phobic users, who may be surprised by the ease of use — and general uselessness — of Recorder, the resident Windows macro program. To be fair, it's only a demo program, and the fact that it does little more than automatically stamp text shouldn't be held against it.

But if you are serious about automation — even on the simplest level — it pays to replace Recorder with something more potent. A good choice is ProKey for Windows, a version of the venerable DOS macro utility. You can automate routine tasks as *global* — across the Windows environment — or specific to a certain application. Each macro has its own "floating" key that you can place anywhere on the screen; click it to start the macro.

Everyone can find some use for ProKey. While you are climbing aboard the Windows boat, it makes sense to leave the macrophobia on the dock — unless you want to end up doing the same things, over and over.

CHAPTER 6

## ▶ Time waits for no one

> Besides showing you the time, you can set audible or written alarms with any of several different clocks.

As you've seen in previous chapters, "virtual" is an important word in the Wonderful World of Windows. It makes sense, therefore, to describe the Windows Clock, which can make the amazing jump from analog to digital, as virtually useless. It is, in fact, a good example of how a computer program can add absolutely nothing to the "real world" application it reflects.

There are ways to keep time with Windows that are worth using — replacements for the virtually useless clock — but they are usually part of other packages. For instance, hDC's First Apps features an alarm clock that sends audible or written signals at predetermined times. Here, you can trigger a dialogue box to remind you to start taping "Bedazzled" off HBO at 11:15. Another trusty timekeeper comes as part of Aristosoft's Wired for Sound. Talking Clock has a variety of cute alarms and speaks the time through your PC's speaker — a sound so distorted that you'll probably end up relying on the wall clock.

## ▶ Windows communications packages don't have to be Terminal

> Terminal is adequate for beginning telecommunications, but there are many better alternatives. The best solution right now is to use a DOS communications product.

Terminal is one of the applets that comes with Windows. It's a good, basic telecommunications program, useful for logging on to CompuServe or BIX and picking up your e-mail. But if you want to do anything serious, like download a lot of files, Terminal really doesn't have it together.

Terminal is not the be-all and end-all of communications. Like the other applets, it's just enough to get you started. However, many of Terminal's apparent shortcomings really belong to Windows: communications via modem just isn't very good under Windows. All those lovely screens and graphics tend to slow Windows down when it tries to scroll large quantities of text.

Some of the best Windows communications packages are CrossTalk for Windows, DynaComm (made by Future-Soft, who also wrote Terminal), and WinComm. These have a lot more features than Terminal, but fall short of popular DOS communications shareware such as Qmodem and Telix (Windows versions are planned for both programs). If you're pushing the envelope on features, you may have to use Qmodem or Telix until Windows communication programs catch up.

## ▶ What's a Modem?

To communicate with another computer, you'll need to get a *modem*. A modem (a rather ugly word that is a contraction for *modulator-demodulator*) is connected to your computer and turns the digital pulses from the computer into sounds that it can transmit over a phone line. A modem at the other end of the phone line listens to these tones and turns them back into digital pulses, which are then interpreted by the computer the second modem is connected to. The effect is almost like having a keyboard with a very long extension cord — the information you type on your keyboard goes into the computer at the other end of the line, and you see the results on your monitor.

Modems are rated by their speed. The most popular modem speed right now is 2400 bits per second or baud (a technical term commonly used interchangeably with bits per second), but 9600 baud modems are becoming relatively inexpensive. 2400 baud is good enough for most purposes while you're learning. Look for a modem that will do auto-answer (you can tell it to pick up the phone) and is "Hayes-compatible." Hayes Microcomputer Products, Inc., has set the standard for modems and how they work.

## ▶ Who ya gonna call?

> You can use your favorite communications program and your modem to call online information services and bulletin boards (BBSes). CompuServe's free demonstration account is a good place to experiment.

Some of the most common things to do with a communications program are logging on to online information services like CompuServe, BIX, and GEnie, or to local bulletin boards (generally known as BBSes). You can also share files directly with someone across town or across the country by connecting your computer to theirs directly over the phone lines. This can be fast and convenient — the long-distance charges you might incur are a fraction of the cost of express mail and it gets there right away.

CompuServe, the world's largest online information service, has a free demonstration account. You can dial CompuServe as a local call from all major cities in the US. For information on the local number for your area, phone CompuServe's Customer Service representatives at 800-848-8990 (617-457-8600 inside Ohio). For bulletin board numbers in your area, check local computer stores or *Computer Shopper* magazine.

For more information on bulletin boards and online information services, get *Using Computer Bulletin Boards* by John Hedtke. The book is designed to introduce novices to computer bulletin board systems and basic telecommunications, and to help intermediate and advanced BBS users to use BBSes more effectively. (Blatant plug!)

## ▶ Just the fax, Ma'am

> You can add a fax card to your computer and have complete fax capabilities for far less than you'd spend on a fax machine. Fax cards even do Windows now.

Fax — the ability to transmit facsimile documents and images across telephone lines — is one of the most convenient and universal ways to transmit information. You can take a file from a PC and send it to any location around the world. The recipient doesn't need to have a computer. In effect, every fax machine becomes a printer.

A fax card in your computer lets you send and receive just like a regular fax machine. Windows, when used with a fax program, makes sending and receiving faxes almost seamless. You can combine text, pictures, and graphs in a document, then select the "Print" command and a phone number to send on-screen images cross-country.

The big drawback with fax cards is that you can't send anything that hasn't been converted into a computer file. This means that you can't send a cartoon you just clipped, someone's resume, or a copy of a letter with the signature unless you can scan it into the computer with a scanner or by sending it from a standard fax machine that does scan. However, many people find that this is outweighed by the convenience of working with Windows. Character-recognition software is also becoming cheaper and easier to find, making it possible to convert a faxed document into a text file that you can then edit in Word for Windows.

For the time being, the best deal comes from Intel and its $399 SatisFAXion board. Not only does it excel in service, support and construction, but FAXit — a superior Windows fax utility — comes free with the board (Figure 6-4).

**FUN AND FUNCTIONAL**

**Figure 6-4**
With FAXit, fax options pop up through the Print menu.

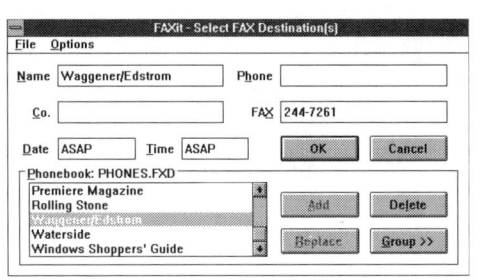

CHAPTER 6

# Control Boxing

Every window in Windows has a control box, a small, grey area in its upper left-hand corner. Accessible either by the mouse or the Alt-Spacebar command, the control box universally lets you minimize and maximize windows, and close and switch applications. This is useful, necessary — and dull.

Dullness aside, the control box has become the avenue to expand the Windows command set. There are only so many things that can be done with pull-down menus. Granted, with ten selections in eight groups, there's room for a lot of commands. But pull-downs necessarily group functions in a strict manner — File, Edit, and so on, necessitating a place for all the commands that's universal, or that don't fit in any one category.

The control box, then, becomes a command orphanage, a place where menus go when they don't fit anywhere else. With more third-party software merchants using this option, selecting this dull little box may lead you into a command wonderland.

You can expect vendors of Windows utility software to stake a claim on the control box, as it's one of the system's most accessible and universal aspects. However, you need to be careful about which programs occupy this new real estate. For instance, installing several such programs would cause the open control box to cover about half the screen. Also, if you have a lot of submenus, it'll take a while to remember where everything is located.

For these reasons, a souped-up control box isn't for everybody; it tends to place another level of complexity between Windows and you. On the other hand, it gives you more power over your computing destination, and, true to its name, increases the control over your system.

Control box applications usually employ cascading submenus, an option absent in most first-generation Windows 3.0 applications. This emphasizes a "folding" effect, and multiplies the amount of possible options. While the number of possible submenus is infinite, too many will make things confusing — actually defeating Windows'

## FUN AND FUNCTIONAL

prime directive — so submenus are associated with what comes before, just like pull-downs. The presence of submenus is usually indicated by a indicator to the right of the menu item. After you memorize a particular sequence, you can zip through it with keyboard commands.

The products in this section all enhance or expand on the basic functions in the control box. We'll be talking about:

- hDC's line of Microapps
- WinConnect, a Windows version of LapLink from Traveling Software
- Several different product launchers, including PCTools and Norton Desktop for Windows

## hDC-It

> hDC's Microapps expand the control box dramatically. Perhaps the best feature is Auto Save.

The pioneer of control box exploration is hDC Computer Corp., of Redmond, WA. hDC has developed a line of "Microapps" that are accessible from the control box. While the standard control box has only the basics, installing both FileApps and FirstApps packages gives you a variety of functions at your fingertips. This ranges from the essential — the manipulation of files and information about the system — to the frivolous: the creation of substitute icons and the installation of animated wallpaper.

Ingeniously, hDC has brought the bug-filled DOS concept of memory residence into the Windows world. Like DOS utilities, Microapps are accessible from within any application at any time. If you need to copy a file or check a memory level you just click the appropriate command in the control box. Unlike DOS utilities, you don't need to worry about conflicts, interrupts, or which utility to load first. And true to the nature of Windows menus, only a single click or an Alt-letter combination is needed to get things started.

While it's possible to run file managers concurrently with other applications, the convenience of having file manipulation built into the control box cannot be underestimated. For instance, you may be working on a letter to a friend and want to include a joke passed on by a colleague. The only thing you can remember is that it's embedded in an Excel spreadsheet somewhere and contains the word "macaroon." File Search, from within the control box, will get you there in seconds flat (this function can also be applied to more businesslike uses).

While most will find something useful in hDC's basket of tricks, there's one utility that qualifies as being absolutely essential. Auto Save (Figure 6-5) can be configured to save changes to disk at specified intervals, so, in the event of an emergency, only the most recent data will be lost.

**FUN AND FUNCTIONAL**

**Figure 6-5**
hDC's Auto Save lets you time file save for the active window.

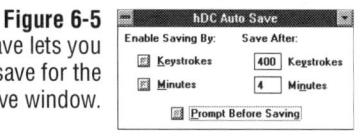

This feature will be most important to the new Windows user. It also may be the best reason to purchase Micro-Apps when you buy your system. While there is no scientific reason or statistical proof for this, a Windows novice is subject to more crashes, freezes, and glitches than someone who's been Windowing for a while. Unless you plan to take six weeks off for training, an Auto Save module has the potential to save more than your data.

A word of caution: Auto Save only saves the active window, and has no effect on minimized applications. For this reason, it's smart to run a quick save (Alt-F-S) before minimizing any window. Along with the image, this minimizes the chances that you'll be in deep yogurt if the system crashes.

When you install hDC Microapps, they become accessible through each window's control box. This turns the box red, with a yellow hDC company logo superimposed on the face. Even the most ardent hDC fans may tire of such plugola. To go commercial-free, do the following:

**1.** Use an ASCII editor to open HDC.INI, in the Windows subdirectory.

**2.** Find the [hDC MicroApp Manager] section of the file.

**3.** Add the following lines, with a numerical value for each color. (Both sets of values must be the same.)
```
Icon Foreground Color=[Red value] [Green value] [Blue value]
Icon Background Color=[Red value] [Green value] [Blue value]
```

> **Note** This procedure lets you do a heretofore impossible "little thing," as Windows only allows flat grey as a color option for the control box.

175

## ▶ Link it

*Traveling Software's WinConnect lets you access hard drives and data on other computers as if they were part of your own.*

While hDC hopes to develop Microapps into a platform, there have been too few takers so far. One, however, has been Traveling Software, which has developed a basic connectivity product that goes beyond their standard LapLink product. Dubbed WinConnect, it lets you patch two computers together through the serial port and access and manipulate files between them. A desktop computer running Word for Windows can update a XyWrite file that was created on a laptop or other computer, then save it back to the original disk.

By necessity, the remote drive accessed by WinConnect will always be slower than your local drive. Still, this is a good way to connect two computers for elementary file exchange and will minimize the pre-trip runaround looking for the right files to take on the road.

▶ **Note** Long-time fans of Traveling Software's LapLink will be pleased to hear that the newest version, LapLink Pro, now does Windows. LapLink Pro also lets you dial into a remote computer and access files, even if the remote computer doesn't have a copy of LapLink Pro installed on it at the time!

## ▶ Let's do launch

> Besides hDC, others products such as Central Point Software and Norton Desktop for Windows are using the Control Box. Right On! even lets you launch apps with your mouse.

hDC is not the only company to add value to the control box. Applications launchers, which allow you to associate startup commands and assign them to control box items, are available as part of PC Tools Version 7.0 and the Norton Desktop for Windows. You can trigger the Notepad, File Manager, or any other commonly used program with a single point and click.

Furthermore, you can achieve a new level of launch pizzazz by associating files with launch commands. For instance, if you use CrossTalk for Windows to check MCI Mail, type the following into the command-line box (don't type "[space]" — press the space bar):

```
\windows\xtalk\xtalk.exe [space]
\windows\xtalk\xwp\mci.xwp
```

When this item is selected off the launch menu, it automatically connects to MCI Mail. So you can check your mailbox from within any other application.

Using both Central Point and Norton launchers may be a luxury that few can afford, but it adds a level of convenience; with two different launchers, you can group program types and develop a detailed submenu structure.

The Norton Desktop for Windows takes the launch concept a step further by providing a Task List item on the control box menu, allowing you to select any open application. A Task List option, in conjunction with a launcher, makes it possible to go anywhere in Windows from anywhere else. This ability is one of the little things that makes Norton Desktop a great program. It's a shame that such a utility isn't more affordable.

Finally, Fanfare Software's mouse utility, Right On!, accesses its configuration through a control box menu. This lets you reprogram the middle and right mouse buttons from within any application. This is a convenience, as it lets you remap mouse buttons from anywhere in the system.

## CHAPTER 6

## Mini Review: The hDC Power Launcher

In the world of control boxing, hDC's Power Launcher (Figure 6-6) is a little like Muhammad Ali — except that Ali has retired, whereas this program is ready to go for a quick three rounds with the competition.

**Figure 6-6**
hDC's Power Launcher lets you customize the control box menus.

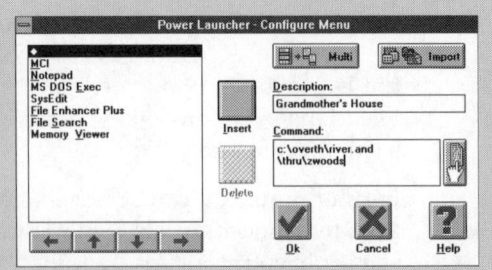

Power Launcher's charter is that the control box should control all system aspects. Here, you can build your own specialized system menus, where all your applications are available from within any other. File association takes things a step further. You could place the document or spreadsheet of the day on the menu and change it as soon as the project is finished.

Power Launcher's utilities include a Task List and a virtual desktop, a less fancy version of WideAngle. The program isn't a pushover. It requires you to plan what you want out of the system and experiment to develop a workable menu sequence. While Power Launcher isn't for everybody, it helps manage the higher level that many Windows users now inhabit.

With the incorporation of Microapps, Power Launcher allows you to build a complete system control panel from the control box. It includes such features as a system information gauge and timed events. For a select group it'll supply the best part of Norton Desktop for Windows at about half the price. In fact, Power Launcher installation as the system shell provides a minimalist option, a fast way for people who know where they are going to reach their destination. On the Windows seas, Power Launcher is a speedboat.

# Window Boxing

This selection is a potpourri of odd and unusual programs. Nothing special, really, but they're useful. Learn how to:

- Customize your cursor
- Compress files from within Windows
- Add sound to your PC
- Use Wired for Sound for Mac-like sound effects
- Program your PC to talk to you with Monologue for Windows

# CHAPTER 6

## ▶ Cursors, foiled again!

> If you really haven't anything better to do with your time, you can always mess with the shape of your cursor.

The Windows cursor is an expressive little beast. While it always follows the locus of mouse control, it also shows some indication of system options. For instance, when it resembles an arrow you can execute a command, and when it resembles a thin capital "I," it's ready to do something with text. When the system is occupied it assumes the shape of an hourglass, which some applications even allow you to watch sand trickle through it.

As expressive as it may be, this little digital animal may be hard to spot in some situations (this is perhaps truer on a laptop, but "normal" desktop users share the problem). The solution is to replace the standard cursor with something more animate.

Shareware cursor programs, available from bulletin boards and user groups, offer a great variety of weird shapes. You can simply substitute a larger arrow, or use a tiny representation of Boris Badenov or Calvin and Hobbes. This is fun, diverting stuff; a personal touch on par with monogrammed golf balls. And the programs have an innate sense of humor — one even pops up a #@#& sequence in the active window. ("Curse-er," get it?)

Dumbness, however, can be counterproductive. Some of these symbols are patently unusable because they flout a basic principle: the cursor is intended to point, and a round head (cute as it may be) isn't exactly a capable pointing device. You'll find this out the first time you try to enlist Boris' help for a File Save.

True to form, to get something done right, you need to pay. The $49 Magic Cursor (Figure 6-7) has about 40 options, like sized arrows, crosshairs, grids, and hands. All have an obvious focal point, and all make the cursor easier to see.

**FUN AND FUNCTIONAL**

**Figure 6-7**
Magic Cursor offers several ways to make your point.

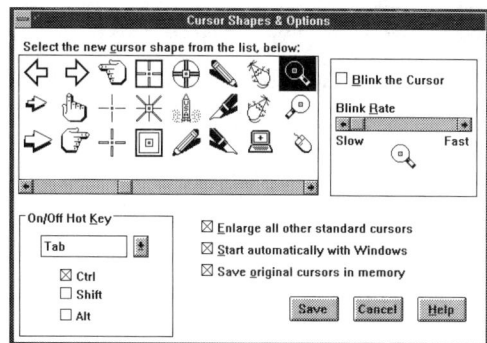

Cursor modification is the next potential arena for ridiculous Windows tricks. Some vendors have threatened the obvious next step, installing a paint-style control that lets you design your own cursor. Expect this option to be available soon. Such fine-tuning is worthwhile up to a point: the person who spends two hours designing the perfect cursor is probably related to the guy who uses calligraphy to customize his golf balls.

## ▶ Zip-a-dee-doo-dah

> Compression utilities, such as WINUNZIP and Stacker, can keep your disk space at a maximum.

While not quite as valuable as Manhattan real estate, hard disk space shouldn't be wasted — especially under Windows, where graphical images can take 1 MB each, and there's the added temptation to join the utility-of-the-month club. For this reason, a well-tempered Windows environment will include a utility to pack and unpack files, allowing you to store data and applications you may not use every day.

A packing utility, like the shareware WINUNZIP, won't be appropriate for instant retrieval of compressed files in the same way as complete compression utilities like Stacker. On the other hand, it lets you turn a corner of a hard disk into a digital wall safe, where you can keep one or more files for eventual retrieval. While there's no security involved, either in protecting the file's contents or preventing accidental erasure, a compression utility can add a level of convenience at a low cost — basically the price of an icon on the desktop.

## ▶ The sound of one PC clapping

> You don't have to get into multimedia to enjoy sound on your PC. Several programs give you sounds and even speech.

Multimedia is the new buzzword of the decade. In a few years, your PC will be able to do all kinds of neat things that we can only imagine today. Consider the first 10 years of the PC. We had only our eyes and hands to deal with PCs. Now, a blast: sound is here to stay.

There are a few ways to harness the PC's sound capabilities through Windows without going "multimedia" and buying into an expensive upgrade. You can expect the "new dimension" of computing to weather the typical initial glitches, so you might want to stay out of harm's way at first, amusing yourself with silly noises while the rest of the world volunteers as multimedia guinea pigs.

There are two kinds of "non-multimedia" Windows applications: those claiming to need additional hardware support and those claiming to make do with the installed PC speaker. It's important to remember that the latter claim is, under all circumstances, impossible. The PC's speaker is a useless piece of metal that is only good for modem squawks and warning beeps. Even for this it may be lacking.

In order to hear what a PC is saying, some kind of enhancement is needed. This can be through an expansion card like the Sound Blaster or a parallel port add-in like M.P. Technologies' Sound Booster. Wariness is suggested. Remember that the same person who claims a program is audible through a second-rate solution is probably related to the guy who says Windows can run on an XT.

CHAPTER 6

## ▶ Sometimes you feel like a Mac

*Wired for Sound gives you a variety of sounds through your PC's speaker.*

If you don't really need to understand the sounds the PC makes, the internal speaker will do. Take Wired for Sound (Figure 6-8), a $49 utility that assigns various effects to system functions: a doorbell can be assigned to the system opening, while a UAE will be the cue for a bomb blast. In the "useful" category, it signals errors to people who issue "Print" commands and walk away.

**Figure 6-8**
Wired for Sound gives your PC the sonic range of a barnyard.

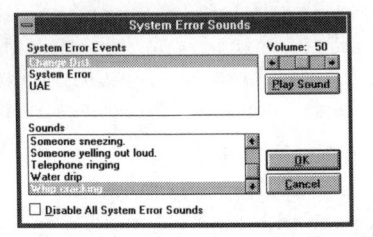

Adding grunts, squeals, and belches to the PC is something that has absolutely no value, aside from making you laugh, which is Windows' big secret. People have been using PCs for a decade, and now they're bored. A little flatulence is needed to liven things up, and DOS just doesn't cut it. Many people, faced with the choice between Wired for Sound and something actually "useful," will go for the gusto. Wired for Sound also won't leave you high and dry with the same old noises. There are plans for a sound library on CompuServe and a service to digitize and convert custom passages for the Wired environment.

The problem with Wired for Sound originates again with the poor speaker quality: in some cases, the belches are barely identifiable. There are a few things you can do: Wired for Sound doesn't support the Sound Blaster, although it will be enhanced by parallel port boosters such as the Disney Box. More enterprising folks will just replace the internal speaker with a larger one — 3½ inches should do the trick.

## Speak thy piece

> Monologue for Windows is a speech synthesis program. There's no inflection, though, so it can't do good Shakespeare readings yet.

Like Wired for Sound, Monologue for Windows claims to work without hardware enhancement. Don't try it. Monologue, a speech synthesis program, needs to be understood. Monologue isn't as much fun as Wired for Sound, but it can be funnier. After selecting a block of text or numbers, the program spits them out in perfect computerese. Monologue? More like Monotone.

The process is ingenious, even if the uses are somewhat prosaic. With a right-button mouse signal, Monologue will repeat the contents of the Clipboard. You'll need a sound card to make it intelligible; even then the emotionless tone will be disconcerting. Even so, it could develop into a useful writer's tool: if all feeling is stripped from the voice, it's easier to see weaknesses in the writing and eliminate them.

CHAPTER 6

# And Now, the Moment You've All Been Waiting For

So far, we've focused largely on ways to make Windows easier to use. Oh, there've been a few things that weren't completely justifiable, like tweaking your icons and playing with your cursor, but most of this book has been aimed at helping you to be more productive.

We're now going to set that aside for a few moments and tell you how to have pure, unadulterated, time-wasting fun with the following Windows products:

- Finding the brag screens in Windows products
- Cheating at Solitaire and Minesweeper
- Saving your screen with After Dark
- Using WinFish to turn Windows into an aquarium
- Playing Castle of the Winds, a great new computer dungeoning game

## Digital graffiti

> Hidden in the deep recesses of many Windows programs are brag screens — the names of the people who helped create the product.

The signatures of the original Apple Macintosh development team were embossed on the inside of each case. Similarly, Microsoft credited more than 100 unsung individuals and embedded their names into Windows and other Windows applications. There are a few differences between the Apple and Microsoft gestures, reflecting perhaps the change in times and the difference between hardware and software. Or maybe it's just that Microsoft doesn't sanction putting credits into programs, so the developers have to be a little sneaky about it.

To see the list of credits for Windows 3.0, switch to the desktop and type WIN3 as you hold down the F3 key. Then release F3 and press Backspace once. (Be sure you minimized your Program Manager; the credits replace your wallpaper.) You'll see a list of the e-mail IDs of the Win 3.0 developers.

The brag screen for Windows 3.1 is much more impressive. Start by switching to the Program Manager. Hold down the Ctrl and Shift keys, then do the following:

1. Click on About Program Manager at the bottom of the Help menu.

2. Double-click the Windows 3.1 icon.

3. Click on OK.

The About box disappears. (You're still holding the Ctrl and Shift keys down.)

4. Click on About Program Manager at the bottom of the Help menu, again.

5. Double-click the Windows 3.1 icon, again.

You'll see a small waving Windows 3.1 flag and a banner (Figure 6-9).

## CHAPTER 6

**Figure 6-9**
Windows 3.1 tips its hat to the development team in a small way.

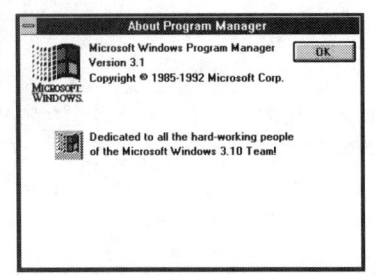

**6.** Click on OK

The About box disappears a second time. (Don't release the Ctrl and Shift keys, yet.)

**7.** Click on About Program Manager at the bottom of Help, a third time.

**8.** Double-click the Windows 3.1 icon.

This time, you'll see a window open up in the About box and one of several figures will point proudly to a slowly scrolling list of names. You can interrupt the procedure by pressing ESC.

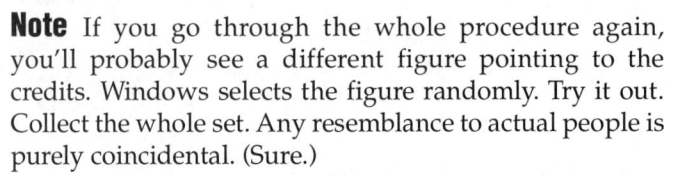

> **Note** If you go through the whole procedure again, you'll probably see a different figure pointing to the credits. Windows selects the figure randomly. Try it out. Collect the whole set. Any resemblance to actual people is purely coincidental. (Sure.)

Windows is not the only program with hidden credits. For example, Excel 3.0's brag screen is animated. From a new sheet in Excel 3.0, select the word "Normal" in the status tool bar and change it to "Excel." Now hold down the shift key and drag the scroll bars all the way to the right so that you have just the last cell (IV16384) visible. Change the column width and row height to 0 (it's probably easiest to do this with the mouse). Click twice on the cell and the credits roll. The animation was modelled after "Bambi Meets Godzilla."

Excel 4.0 doesn't have individual credits, but it does have a very interesting animated sequence, showing Excel 4.0 dealing with a competitor. According to highly placed — and anonymous — sources at Microsoft, maximize Excel and add the "solitaire" button (the custom macro button

## FUN AND FUNCTIONAL

with a deck of cards on it) to any toolbar, but don't attach a macro to it. Cancel and close everything until you get back to the toolbar. Maximize the sheet, then hold down Ctrl and Shift and click the Solitaire button. No problemo!

None of these will prepare you for the credits in Word for Windows. Getting the brag screen in Word for Windows 1.1 is a fairly elaborate process:

1. Set the Caps Lock button on.
2. Select Define Styles from the Format menu. Normal should be the default style in the box that appears.
3. Click Options.
4. In the "Based on" box, select Normal from the list.
5. Click OK. You'll get an error message that says a style can't be based on itself.
6. Click Cancel.
7. Click About on the Help menu.
8. Type OPUS (WinWord's 1.1 original code name), being sure to hold down each key.

What follows is a firework-tinged scrolling of e-mail IDs that goes on for some time, sort of like movie credits that list everyone from the caterer to the kennelmeister. If this particular feature adds nothing to the program and would be impossible to find without a roadmap, it still adds an amusing personal touch to the Microsoft suite of applications.

Not only is Word for Windows 2.0's brag screen fancier, it's much easier to reach (some people felt that the procedure for getting the brag screen in Word for Windows 1.1 was just a *little* too elaborate):

1. Select Macro from the Tools menu.
2. Create a macro called SPIFF.
3. Delete all the text in the macro.
4. Close the macro box and save the SPIFF macro.
5. Go to the Help menu and select About.

## CHAPTER 6

**6.** Click on the Word for Windows icon to start the demonstration (Figure 6-10).

**Figure 6-10**
Word for Windows 2.0 addresses the competition.

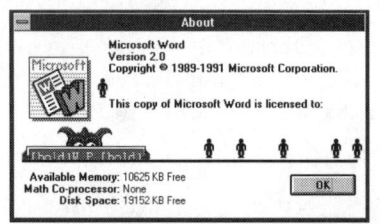

Some EGA and some large screen monitors may have trouble showing the little guy running around and beating up the WP monster, but everyone gets to see the fireworks and the credits that follow.

Interestingly enough, if you save the SPIFF macro as a global macro, you can see the brag screen anytime you click on the icon in the About box. The program is just looking for the existence of the macro rather than a specific set of keystrokes and actions.

Other Microsoft programs — and other Windows programs, too — have brag screens. Keep an eye on the PC gossip columns; someone will talk sooner or later.

# The Microsoft Entertainment Packs

*The games in the Microsoft Entertainment Packs are the perfect solution to fill all that extra time you've saved.*

Windows 3.0 contained two games, Solitaire and Reversi. Reversi had been part of Windows since Windows 1.0, but Solitaire was new — and very popular. Many users wrote Microsoft to say it was their favorite feature in version 3.0.

To capitalize on the enormous popularity of the games in Windows 3.0, Microsoft released a package of Windows games shortly after Windows 3.0 came out. The sales were incredible, so Microsoft released two more game packs in the fall of 1991. Minesweeper, one of the games in the first Microsoft Entertainment Pack, proved so popular that it made it into the release version of Windows 3.1.

### Who dealt this mess, anyway?

Solitaire has hundreds of versions. The one that Wes Cherry wrote is known as Klondike or Canfield. It's been the most popular single-player game since the 1920s.

You probably know how to play Solitaire already. What you probably *don't* know is that you can cheat. If you're playing drawing three cards at a time and you need that *one* card in the middle of a group, try holding down Ctrl-Alt-Shift and then click on the draw pile. Instead of drawing the next three cards, you'll only draw one. When you release the keys, you draw three cards again just like always. This doesn't show up on your score, by the way, so no one will know. Pretty sneaky, eh?

### Watch where you're stepping!

In Minesweeper, the object of the game is to find out which squares in a field have mines under them. Sounds simple enough, but the way you find out is by stepping on them. If the square doesn't blow up, you get to try again. If it does, well....

Minesweeper's author, Rob Donner, graciously revealed his mine-detection system. Start by moving all your windows, including the Program Manager, over so that there's nothing on the upper left-hand corner of the desktop. Start Minesweeper, but just move the mouse pointer over the minefield. Now type xyzzy and press Enter, then press Shift once. Move the mouse pointer across a couple of squares and watch the upper left-hand corner of the screen carefully. When you're pointing to a square that doesn't have a mine under it, you'll see a tiny white dot (one pixel). If the square covers a mine, the dot is black.

You can turn the mine detector off by pressing Shift again. But even if you leave it on, your friends probably won't know what to look for. However, you shouldn't bet really *large* amounts of money on your ability to wend your way through minefields — they may have read this book, too!

**Other ways to waste your time**
The Microsoft Entertainment Packs contain a variety of games that will suit every taste, including:

- TETRIS, a popular Macintosh game, now on Windows
- FujiGolf, a golf game set at the Mt. Fuji golf course
- Golf, Cruel, Tut's Tomb, FreeCell, and TriPeaks, exciting solitaire card games
- IdleWild, a screen saver with different modules

You can buy the Microsoft Entertainment Packs at any retail software outlet. If you're interested in finding out more about the games (along with a lot of inside information on how to cheat), you can buy a copy of *Winning! The Awesome and Amazing Insider's Book of Windows Game Tips, Traps, and Sneaky Tricks*, by John Hedtke. (Yet another blatant plug!)

# FUN AND FUNCTIONAL

## ▶ Blank expression

*After Dark is a collection of screen savers every Windows user should have.*

After Dark (Figure 6-11) comes from Berkeley Systems in Berkeley, CA. In early 1989, a physics grad student named Jack Eastman wanted to try some programming on the Mac. He decided to do a modular screen saver, one that would do about six different things. When he was done, he showed it to Berkeley Systems, who liked it so much they added a lot of modules and sold it as a Mac product. Version 2.0 for the Mac came out in late summer of 1990, and included Fish (which is discussed later in this chapter) and the wildly-popular Flying Toasters.

**Figure 6-11**
The After Dark control panel.

The Windows version of After Dark came out at the beginning of 1991 and it was stunning. Berkeley Systems released After Dark for Windows 2.0 in early 1992 to equally rave reviews. Some of the features in 2.0 include digitized sound, a capture utility, and lots of improvements to existing modules. People who have super VGA monitors and cards will be particularly impressed by the colors in the new version.

After Dark for Windows 2.0 costs $49.95 and is available at most computer stores.

# CHAPTER 6

## ▶ A tail of two fishes

> One of the most popular screen savers for Windows and the Macintosh is Fish (also known as "Codview for Windows").

Ed Fries likes fish. I mean, he *really* likes fish. His office is full of fish mobiles, fish posters, fish toys, and there's even an old terminal that's been turned into an aquarium. Everyone else is aware that he likes fish, too. One time, when Ed was away, people used 2800 paper cups full of water and food coloring to create a giant bit mapped fish on his floor (each cup was a pixel). The water leaked through the paper cups and there's now the ghost of a bit-mapped fish permanently visible in Ed's carpet. On another occasion, Ed's good buddies built a giant papier-mache fish in his office that (naturally) was too big to fit through the door.

Ed created a simple program for Windows 1.0 of fish swimming as an exercise in Windows programming. It used icons for swimming fish. When Windows 2.0 came out, Ed created a much better version that was very popular at his company, but was not officially released or sold. There was also a demo version with a sub that hunted down and blew up the fish as they swam that was very popular with the product marketers.

Tom Saxton, an expert in Macintosh programming, had heard of Ed and of WinFish. Tom created the first version of a fish editor that let you add new fish. The editor and a ported version of Fish became MacFish 1.0. Tom and Ed uploaded the program on CompuServe as freeware. They put the name "Bogus Software" in as a joke. To their surprise, they started getting about one check a month. At the end of a year, they had received a 5-pound note and $100 in checks made out to Bogus Software.

Tom went to the Apple Technology conference in 1988. He mentioned Fish and everyone got very excited. The editor of MacWorld asked if Tom wanted to be featured in a Christmas article. It seemed like a good idea, so they called the company "Tom and Ed's Bogus Software." The Seattle Chamber of Commerce even invited them to join.

## FUN AND FUNCTIONAL

Today, Fish is available in both Windows and Macintosh versions. Fish is also included in After Dark (mentioned earlier in this chapter), the screen saver from Berkeley Systems. One technical writer at Microsoft in the Languages division is passionately fond of WinFish, calling it "Codview for Windows."

Fish works beautifully under Windows 3.1 (Figure 6-12). For $24.95, you get a copy of the WinFish program, 60 fish, and a fish editor so you can create your own fish. (MacFish is $19.95, plus $3.00 shipping and handling.) You can send checks or money orders (no credit card orders) to Tom and Ed's Bogus Software, "101 Windows Tips," 15600 NE 8th, Suite A-3334, Bellevue, WA 98008.

**Figure 6-12**
The fish editor at work: "Salmon chanted evening!"

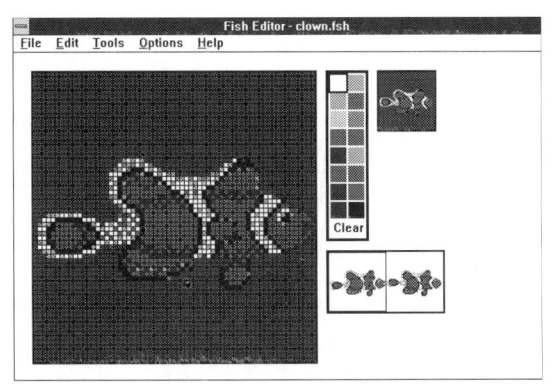

195

## ▶ A king's castle is his home

> We've saved the best for last. Castle is a terrific dungeoning adventure set against a backdrop of Norse mythology.

Rick Saada, noted international playboy, juggler, and generally nice guy, wanted to get off the project he was working on... bad. There were a lot of interesting career paths at the company he worked for, and Rick figured that adding Windows programming to his resume would help him make the switch. At the time, he was playing a lot of Rogue (a character-based dungeoning adventure), so he started writing a dungeoning game in Windows. Strictly as an exercise in programming, you understand. He called it Castle of the Winds, or "Castle" for short.

The very first version of Castle was for Windows 2.0 and was pretty cheesy, largely because of the EGA level graphics. (When Rick later switched to Windows 3.0, the VGA graphics looked much better.) At first, most of the effort was aimed at building good dungeon levels. There weren't many monsters, and there wasn't much plot to the game. The hard part was designing an algorithm for getting plausible, random dungeon levels

After he got the dungeon graphics running smoothly, Rick started expanding on the game. The original half dozen monsters expanded to close to a hundred. The plotline expanded and changed. As the release of Castle 1.0 came near in mid-1992, Rick worked with Paul Canniff and Ben Goetter to develop the final graphics and storyline (Figure 6-13).

# FUN AND FUNCTIONAL

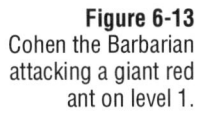

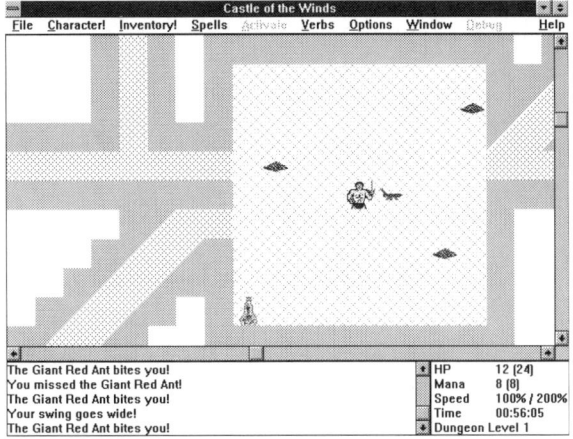

**Figure 6-13**
Cohen the Barbarian attacking a giant red ant on level 1.

One of the neat things about Castle is that it's different each time you play it. There are anchor points to the plotline that appear every time (the goal of the game is always to kill Surtur at the bottom of the dungeon and recover a special magic item), but the game is different each time you play.

*Warning* This game is *very* addictive! You can spend hours killing monsters in the depths before you know it.

Castle of the Winds comes in two modules. In the first module, you descend into a mine. Having recovered an amulet from the bottom of the mine, you are ready to go into the dungeon in the second module and face Surtur (from Norse mythology). You can get the first module on bulletin boards and from shareware distributors. When you send $25 plus $2 shipping handling to Epic Mega-Games (10406 Holbrook Drive, Potomac, MD, 20854, 800-788-0787) you receive both modules.

CHAPTER 6

# Summing Up

One of the big advantages to Windows is that it lets your computer life grow and expand where and when you want it. You can swap or upgrade different components without affecting the whole, sort of like a modular stereo system. Utilities, applications, and even system upgrades can be added when you want them, developing an environment that does what you want when you want it.

Multimedia is here. PCs will soon have the ability to speak (hopefully in more than a monotone). At this rate, smell and taste can't be too far behind. Pretty soon, when people look back to the pre-Windows days of the PC, it could be viewed as the Great Silent Age.

If it's not quite as dramatic as, say, the discovery of fire, Windows' appearance does represent a cut-off point for personal computing's evolution. There are a lot of reasons for this — ease of use, memory, pretty colors — but Windows' most potent aspect remains its adaptability. For the first time, users can design a system from the ground up to reflect their needs and styles. And as the category matures, it's less likely you'll run into a brick wall (or, as some may call it, a digital ceiling).

The bottom line is that Windows improves personal computing. It's easy to use and it's fun. Take the time to learn the system, and it'll treat you well.

# INDEX

_DEFAULT.PIF file  68
386 enhanced mode, see
  enhanced mode
386Max  52
640K barrier  48, 49, 90

## A

active window  41, 148,
  151, 175
adding
  apps to ProgMan  5, 58
  crop marks  73
  files to ProgMan  11
  hard disk  99
  icons  11, 127, 153-156
  memory  90, 91
  sounds  179, 183, 184,
    185, 198
  title  43
adjusting PIF settings  39, 40
Adobe Systems  67, 70
Adobe Type Manager  62
After Dark  186, 193, 194-195
alarm clock  160, 166
Aldus  146
Alt key  120-121
AmiPro 2.0  146
Aporia  144
applets  100, 101, 130, 160, 167
application launchers  177,
  178
applications  3, 146
  brag screens in  186,
    187-190
  cycling through  24
  deleting unused  100-101
  exiting  32, 35, 95
  installing  5
  launching  3, 4, 13-31, 42
  loading grouped  124
  locating  124
  maximizing  20, 21, 25
  memory usage  39, 49,
    97, 98
  minimizing  20, 25, 57
  multimedia  183
  resizing  20, 21, 125
  running one at a time  111
  specifying different
    parameters  47
  starting  15, 17-19, 20, 119,
    131, 177

streamlining  95
switching between  123
system menu  22
tiling  21
archiving program  45
Aristosoft  124-125, 166
arranging icons  4, 5, 35
arranging windows  5, 22, 35
ASCII editors  15, 29-30, 31,
  101, 109, 160, 161, 175
assigning a PIF to an icon  43
associating data files  17,
  26-31, 45, 131, 178
Asymetrix  163
Attitash Software  124
Auto Save  174-175
AUTOEXEC.BAT  15, 26, 29,
  49, 50, 65, 70, 81, 90, 96,
  101, 128-133
automatic crop marks  77
automating procedures  165
autostarting
  applications  17-19
  data files  26-31
avoiding disaster  116

## B

background printing  86
backing up  15, 43, 55, 113,
  116, 131
backup files  29, 30
backup software  55, 116
ballpoint mice  106
Baseline Publishing  124
batch files  15, 18, 29, 30, 50,
  59, 65-66, 67, 68-69, 70
BatchWorks  20
baud  168
BBSes  46, 58, 169, 197
Becker Tools  144-145
Berkeley Systems  193, 195
Big Sky  125
bitmaps  99, 101, 136, 139, 162
bits per second  168
Bitstream FaceLift  62
BIX  167, 169
body text  63
Bogus Software  194-195
brag screens  186, 187-190
bulletin boards, see BBSes
buying a hard disk  98, 99
buying more memory  90, 91

## C

caches  49, 109, 110
Calculator  160, 163
Calendar  100, 163
Canniff, Paul  196
Cardfile  85
Castle of the Winds  186,
  196-197
Central Point Software  56,
  116, 177
changing
  data files to icons  27
  directories in File
    Manager  8
  icons  57, 127, 153-156
  Print Manager  86
  screen colors  127, 147-152
  startup screen  127
  system files  127-133
character-recognition
  software  170
cheating at Windows
  games  186, 191-192
checking email  104
checking memory  49
checking the hard disk  49
Cherry, Wes  191
CHESS.BMP  101
CHKDSK  49, 55, 56
Clipboard  90, 92, 101,
  160, 185
Clock  15, 18, 100, 160,
  163, 166
Close Window on Exit  68-69
Closer  32, 34
closing a directory
  window in File
    Manager  7
closing applications  3, 32, 33,
  34, 95
Codview for Windows  194-5
color monitors  122
color patterns, saving  147
colors  127, 131, 147-152, 175
command-line
  parameters  18, 35, 39, 44-47
COMMAND.COM  39, 43
COMMAND.PIF  39
communicating between
  computers  168, 169, 176

199

# INDEX

communications
  software  46, 100, 160, 167, 169
compressing files  45, 101, 179, 182
compressing your disk  55, 56, 98, 102
compression programs  45, 101, 182
CompuServe  167, 169, 184
Computer Shopper magazine  169
computers  17, 18, 22, 76, 103-112, 113, 117, 176
CONFIG.SYS  30, 49, 50, 90, 96, 109, 110, 112, 126, 128-133
configuration files  29, 30
configuring fonts  63
consolidating groups  95
Control Box  97, 124, 143, 146, 172-178
Control menu  33, 68
Control Panel  65, 73, 74, 75, 76, 77, 80, 82, 86, 108, 138, 147, 148
controlling printing effects  71
conventional memory  49, 52, 110
COPY command  80, 81
copying
  text  92, 162
  directory to floppy  43
  files  11, 174
  icons  4, 14
CorelDraw  112
corrupting files  55, 56
country code  131
crashing  55
creating custom configurations  18
crop marks  73, 77
CrossTalk  123, 125, 167, 177
Cruel  192
cursor, customizing  179, 180-181
customizing
  application startup  20
  Control Box  178
  cursor  179, 180-181
  macros  24
  mouse buttons  119, 177
  Windows  127-157, 179-185
  Windows logo  136
cutting text  92, 162

cycling through applications  24

## D

data
  compression  102, 182
  compression utilities  105, 182
  files  3, 17, 18, 22, 24, 26-31, 44, 45, 178
  loss prevention  116
databases  33
decompression program  45, 182
default shell  35
default tint patterns  83
defragmenting your disk  55, 56, 98, 102
delaying printing  87
deleting applets  100-101, 160
deleting files  100-101
deleting icons  4, 94-95
Designer  71
designing colors  147, 148
designing icons  153-156
DeskJet printer  65, 87
desktop  5, 21, 23, 54, 57, 123, 130, 143
Desktop for Windows  129, 146, 177, 178
desktop publishing  62, 91
DeskTopSet  146, 160, 163-164
device drivers  52-53, 131
device independence  61
dialer  163-164
digital pulses  168
Digital Research  52
digitizing sounds  184
directory windows  6
directory, setting startup  20
disabling Print Manager  130
disk
  caching  49, 109,110
  compression  55, 56, 98, 102
  printing to  73-77, 85
Disney Box  184
display adapter  122
displaying a directory  10
displaying directory trees  8
dithered colors  150
Donner, Rob  191
DOS applications
  changing while running  41

full-screen  16
installing  58
launching  15-16, 43, 45, 46
minimizing  57
multitasking  59
running  43, 48, 98, 111
specifying different parameters  47
speeding up  39, 40, 41
using  36, 37-59
using batch files with  59
using pop-up utilities with  50
DOS command line  15, 18
DOS commands, 39
DOS communications programs  160, 167
DOS icon  57
DOS memory limitations  48
DOS programs, dangers of  55, 56
DOS prompt  17, 18, 49, 136, 143
DOS tips  54
DOS utilities  174
DOS Word  107
DOS, incorrect version  114
DR-DOS  52
drag and drop  129
dragging files  5, 10
dragging icons  4, 5, 14
Dragon's Eye Software  18, 22, 32, 34
drawing icons  67
drawing programs  71, 91, 100
drivers  49, 52-53, 61, 71, 75, 77, 79, 85, 96
dungeoning games  186, 196-197
DynaComm  167

## E

e-mail  46, 104, 167
Eastman, Jack  193
ECHO command  67
editing batch files  18, 30, 31, 65, 66, 67, 67, 68
editing PIF files  39-47, 51
editing system files  12, 15-16, 64, 112, 133, 142
EGA monitors  122, 190
electronic mail  see e-mail
embedding icons  11
enabling error handling  82
encapsulated PostScript  78, 79

200

# INDEX

End Task button 33
enhanced mode 33, 37, 39, 40, 41, 42, 43, 48, 51, 52-53, 68, 104, 108, 123
enhancing the control box 172-178
Enter key 119, 120-121
Epic MegaGames 197
EPS, *see* encapsulated PostScript
erasing shortcut keys 42
errors in setup 114
errors, printer 78, 82
errors, signalling 184
Escape key 120-121
Excel 15, 24, 79, 85, 119, 188-189
executable filename 17, 18
executable files 26
executing DOS commands 39
exiting applications 3, 32-35
exiting utilities 35
exiting Windows 22, 35, 55, 68
expanded memory 110
expanding branches in File Manager 6, 7, 10
expansion card 99, 183
exporting EPS files 78, 79
exporting graphics 79
exporting print files 73-77
extended memory 48, 110
extensions 18, 25, 26, 29-30, 31, 39, 45, 50, 64, 67, 100, 101, 131
extra sizes 77

## F

FaceLift 62
Fanfare Software 177
fax 160, 170-171
FAXit 170-171
Feinleib, David 20
FIL file 39
file extensions 18, 25, 26, 29-30, 31, 39, 45, 50, 64, 67, 100, 101, 131
File F/X 142-143
file handling 3
File Manager 3, 12, 26, 27,31, 72, 151, 177
  associating data files 27, 45
  changing directories in 8
  closing a directory window in 7

collapsing branches in 6, 10
copying files in 11
directory windows, tiling 6
displaying a directory in 10
displaying directory trees in 8
expanding branches in 6, 7, 10
keyboard shortcuts 6-9
launching applications 12, 45
mouse moves 10-11
moving files in 10
moving in 8-9
navigating directory trees 8
opening a new directory 6, 10
printing files in 11
replacing Program Manager 12
selecting files in 7, 10
splitting a window in 10
starting applications from 27
switching drives in 6, 10
switching windows in 6
tiling directory windows in 6
using a mouse in 10-11
using as a shell 12, 25, 57
File menu 26, 27, 45, 58
File Name text box 27
File Organizer 144
file types 131
file, printing to a 61
FILE: 74, 75, 77
FileApps 174
filename, executable 17, 18
files
  adding to ProgMan 11
  backing up 116
  compressing 45, 101, 182
  copying 174
  corrupting 55, 56
  deleting unused 100-101
  downloading 58, 61, 63, 64, 70, 71, 72
  dragging 5, 10
  help 100
  printing to 61, 73-77, 85
  sharing 169
  transferring 176
  undeleting 55, 56

viewing properties of 6
filtering graphic images 162
fine-tuning Windows 126
FirstApps 22, 97, 166, 174
Fish 186, 193, 194-195
Flying Toasters 193
font files 64
font groups 72
font handling 61-88
font installation programs 64
Font Installer dialog 65
font rasterizers 62, 87
fonts 131
  configuring 63
  creating custom groups 72
  downloading 61, 62, 63, 64, 65-66, 67, 70, 71, 72, 78, 80, 81
  installing 65-66
  permanent downloading 65
  PostScript 64
  resident 63
  soft 62, 63, 64
foolproofing your system 54
foreground application 41
formatting your hard disk 56
FreeCell 192
freeing memory 92
Fries, Ed 194
frozen programs 41
FujiGolf 192
fun 159, 186-197
function keys 121
FutureSoft 167

## G

games 186, 191-192, 196-197
generic PIF settings 39
GEnie 169
global tasks 165
Goetter, Ben 196
Golf 192
Grammatik 123
graphic file format 78, 79
graphic images 162
graphics 79, 99
gray tones 83
group windows 5, 23, 94
grouping program types 177
groups 11, 14, 17, 23, 27, 35, 58, 95, 113, 115, 116

**201**

# INDEX

## H

hairline rules  71
halftones  83
handling files  3
handling printer errors  78, 82
hard disk expansion card  99
hard disk optimizing
    software  55, 56
hard disk space  88
hard disk
    adding  99
    backing up  55, 116
    buying  98, 99
    cleaning  98, 100-101
    compressing  56, 98, 102
    defragmenting  56, 98, 102
    formatting  56
    logical  112
    maximizing space  103, 105
    optimizing  56, 98, 99, 102, 103
    protecting  56
    recommended
        capacity  99
    simulating  112
    Stacker  105
Hayes Microcomputer
    Products  168
hDC  19, 20, 22, 35, 97, 98, 125, 143, 146, 160, 163, 166, 173, 174-175, 177, 178
HDC.INI  175
HEADER.TXT  81
headers, printing  78, 80, 81
Hedtke, John  169, 192
help  131
help files  100
Help menu  94
Hewlett-Packard printer  87
hidden credits  186, 187-190
hidden icons  34
hidden swap file  108
HIMEM.SYS  112
HotKey  25
hotkeys, see keyboard
    shortcuts
HotWin  46
hourglass  180
HP LaserJet  65, 87
HyperDisk  110
HyperDrive  107

## I

I/O ports  106
Icon Designer  125
Icon Pak  154-155
icon-drawing utility  67
icons  21, 27, 153-156
    adjusting distance
        between  134, 138
    adjusting properties  20
    and OLE applications  11
    arranging  4, 5, 35
    changing  127
    changing data files to  27
    copying  4, 14
    creating  18, 46, 50, 67, 98, 127, 153-156
    custom  57, 95, 115, 116, 156
    default  115
    designing  98, 153-156
    DOS applications  54
    downloading fonts
        with  65-66, 67
    dragging  4, 5, 14
    eliminating  94-95
    embedding  11
    executing DOS
        commands with  39
    hidden  34, 57
    in Program Manager  11, 43, 50
    libraries  153, 154-155, 156
    linking  11
    loading files with  155
    moving to a different
        group  4, 14
    PIF  43
    position  130, 134, 138
    titling  43
identifying available
    memory  48
identifying printer errors  82
IdleWild  192
Imagesetter  71, 83
importing graphic
    images  162
inactive windows  148
increasing performance
    107-112
independent desktop  123
INI files  128-133
initialization files  29, 128-133
installing
    applications  5, 130
    fax  160
    fonts  65-66

MS-DOS Executive
    143-144
printer  75
SysEdit  133
Windows  29
Intel  170
internal speaker  184
international settings  131

## J

JOB files  72
Jones, Keasley  202

## K

key files, backing up  116
keyboard moves in File
    Manager  6-9
keyboard shortcuts  6-9, 13, 24, 25, 33, 39, 42, 120-121
keyboard speed  130
keyboards  119, 120-121
Kitsos, Costas  72

## L

LapLink  173, 176
laptops  103-106, 176
laser printers  62, 64, 65-66, 67, 70, 78, 83
LaserJet printers  65-66, 87
Launch  20, 25, 34, 46
launchers, application  20, 25, 35, 46, 177, 178
launching applications  3, 4, 12, 13-31, 177, 178
    as icons  23
    batch files for  50
    COMMAND.COM  43
    customizing  20
    keyboard shortcuts  13, 25
    macros  20, 24
    multiple applications  13, 14-16, 22, 23, 25
    RunProg  20
    shortcut keys  42
    using mouse buttons  177
    using the StartUp
        group  14, 17, 27, 35
    with data files  17, 18, 22, 26-31
launching data files  3, 26-31, 44

# INDEX

letter extra size  77
limit of DOS command
  line  15, 18
linking icons  11
Linotronic  73, 77, 83
load=  15-16, 19, 27
loading
  files with icons  155
  memory-resident
    utilities  50
  spreadsheets  129
  Windows  50
locating applications  124
logical disks  112
Logitech  106
logo  134, 135, 136
losing data  49, 55

## M

M.P. Technologies  183
MacFish  194-195
Macintosh sounds  179,
  184, 185
macro utility  100
macros  20, 21, 24, 25, 42, 46,
  160, 165
Magic Cursor  180-181
Main group  58
managing icons  153-156
managing system
  resources  48-53, 89-126
manually downloading
  fonts  62, 63, 64, 70, 71, 72
maximizing
  applications  20, 21, 25
  hard disk space  103, 105
  printer speed  63
  resources  40
MCI mail  125, 129, 177
memory blocks  48, 96
memory  37, 48-53, 88, 90-97,
  98, 103, 105, 110
  adding  90, 91, 99
  checking  49
  conflicts  114
  managing  89-126
  maximizing  52-53, 103,
    105  page mapping
    conflicts  114
  monitors  97, 98
  printer  63
  used by an application  39,
    49, 51, 52, 97, 98

memory-resident
  programs  3, 22, 34, 48, 49,
    50, 52, 174
Memory Viewer  90, 97, 98
menu programs  20
menu-based launcher  35, 46
menus  95, 172-178
Metz Task Manager  35,
  142-143
mice  118
Microapps  143, 163, 173,
  174-175, 178
Microsoft  54, 97, 98, 106,
  187-190
Microsoft Entertainment
  Packs  191-192
Microsoft Excel  15, 24, 79, 85,
  119, 188-189
Microsoft Resource
  Toolkit  97, 98
*Microsoft Windows User's
  Guide*  24, 40, 58, 68, 85
Microsoft Word 5.0  46, 50
Minesweeper  186, 191-192
minimizing applications  14,
  19, 20, 25, 57
minimizing ProgMan  4
modems  106, 167, 168
modifying INI files  131
Mom's Software  56
monitoring memory  90,
  97, 98
monitors  118, 122
monochrome colors  152
Monologue for Windows
  179, 185
MoreWindows  124-125
mouse
  alternatives to  106
  buttons  119, 130, 177
  changing speed  131
  drivers  49
  maximizing memory
    with  48
  port  106
  using with Windows  119
mouseless PCs  106
moving applications
  between groups  58
moving files in File
  Manager  10
moving icons to a
  different group  4, 14
moving in File Manager  8-9
MS-DOS 5.0  52, 55, 56
MS-DOS Executive  143-144
multimedia  183, 198

multiple users  17, 18, 22, 76
multitasking  37, 39, 41,
  59, 123-125

## N

naming print files  73, 76
navigating File Manager  8
network drivers  49
newsletters  88
NoDOS  57
Non-Windows
  Applications group  58
Northgate keyboards  121
Norton Desktop for
  Windows  95, 129, 146, 173,
  177, 178
Norton Utilities  56
notebook computers  103-106
Notepad  12, 15, 25, 29, 31,
  65, 76, 101, 109, 128, 130,
  132, 133, 160, 161, 177

## O

Okna  163
OLE applications  11
opening a new directory
  in File Manager  6, 10
opening applications  146
opening the system menu  41
operating environment  3
optimizing memory  103
optimizing your disk  55, 56,
  98, 102, 103
optimizing your system
  89-126
Optional Parameters box  37,
  43, 44-47
Options menu  4, 23, 77, 86
output devices  131
output ports  131
overriding shortcut keys  39
overwriting print files  76

## P

page mapping conflicts  114
PageMaker  17, 26, 77, 83, 112
Paintbrush  101
paper size  77
parallel port  67
parameters  18, 35, 44-47
pasting text  92, 162

**203**

# INDEX

path 27
PATH command 15, 26
PAUSE command 69
PC Magazine 22
PC Tools 56, 116, 145, 173, 177
PCL printer 70
PCSEND 67, 72, 80, 81
pen mice 106
peripherals 88
permanent downloading
 of fonts 65
permanent swap file 107, 108
PFB file 64
phone book 163-164
photographs, scanning 99
PIF Editor 33, 37, 40, 42,
 44-47, 51, 68-69
PIF files 15, 31, 31, 33, 37,
 39-47, 51, 58, 68-69
 creating 46
 decompressing files
  with 45
 editing 51
 launching
  COMMAND.COM
  with 43
 using custom icons
  with 57
 using to back up 43
PIF settings, adjusting 39, 40
PKWare 101
PKZIP 45, 101
plugging in chips 91
pointing devices 103, 106
pop-up programs 20, 50
portable computers 103-106
ports 74, 75, 76, 106, 131
positioning windows 13
PostScript 61, 64, 67, 70, 74,
 78-83
Power Launcher 19, 20, 119,
 125, 143, 146, 178
Preferences menu 95
print files 73-77
print headers 78, 80, 81
Print Manager 11, 50, 77, 84,
 86, 87, 101, 130
printer
 drivers 61, 71, 75, 77, 79, 85
 errors, reporting 78, 82
 font files 64
 memory 63
 ports 74, 131
 ROM 63
printing 61-88
 controlling effects 71
 crop marks 73, 77

delaying 87
files in File Manager 11
for Linotronic output 77
graphic information 85
gray scales 8, 83
headers 78, 80, 81
in Excel 79, 85
in the background 86
newsletters 88
proof pages 84
speeding up 84-87
spreadsheets 88
term papers 88
tints 83
to disk 61, 73-77, 85
with Print Manager 86
problems 113-117
processor chip 103
Procomm Plus 29, 46
PROGMAN.EXE 12, 27, 154
program files, dragging 5
program groups 11, 14, 17,
 23, 27, 35, 58, 95, 113,
 115, 116
program information
 file, see PIF file
program launcher 12, 35, 46
Program Manager 3, 94, 95,
 101, 129, 141, 145, 151
 adding applications to 5
 adding icons to 11, 18, 67
 icons in 154-155
 installing DOS
  applications 58
 keyboard shortcuts in 24
 launching
  applications with 23, 46
 minimizing 4
 PIF icons 43
 Properties dialog box 5,
  14, 18, 20, 27
 rebuilding groups 115
 replacing 12, 127, 141-145
 Run dialog box 24
 StartUp group 14, 17,
  27, 35
 using 4, 35
 using as shell 25, 35, 57
 using Closer with 34
programs see applications
ProKey for Windows 160, 165
prompt 17, 18
proof pages, printing 84
Properties dialog box 5, 14,
 18, 20, 27, 154, 155
protecting your
 computer 54, 56

PSDOWN 71, 80
public domain programs 35
Publishing Technologies 20
PubTech File Organizer 144
pulldown menus 172-178
pure colors 150
purging the Clipboard 92

## Q

QEMM-386 52
QMODEM 167
Qualitas 52
Quarterdeck 52

## R

RAM, see also memory
 chips 91
 drives 86, 107, 112
reading messages 68-69
README files 29, 30
README.WRI 18
rebooting 113, 117
rebuilding groups 113, 115,
 116
receiving faxes 170
recommended hard disk
 capacity 99
Recorder 20, 24, 25, 101
recording macros 20, 24, 160,
 165
removing drivers 96
removing wallpaper 90, 93,
 134, 139-140
replacing
 applets 160, 161, 162,
  163-164, 166
 hard disk 98, 99
 icons 153-156
 ProgMan 12, 127, 141-145
 SysEdit 160, 161
 Task Manager 146
 PC speaker 184
 Windows logo 134, 136
resident fonts 63
resizing applications 20,
 21, 125
Resource Toolkit 97, 98
restarting Windows 12, 70
restarting your computer
 113, 117
Reversi 191
Right On 119, 177
RLE file format 136, 140

204

# INDEX

ROM 63
Room for Windows 125
rulers 95
Run 18, 22
RUN command 20
Run dialog box 24
run= 15-16, 19, 27
running
   batch files 31
   DOS applications 39, 43
RunProg 20

## S

Saada, Rick 196
SatisFAXion board 170
saving color patterns 147
saving macros 24
saving memory 90-97
saving Windows settings 4, 22, 35
saving your work 175
Saxton, Tom 194
scaleable typefaces 87
scanning photographs 99
Scrapbook+ 160, 162
screen
   background 130
   colors 127, 131, 147-152
   coordinates 20
   flicker 151
   fonts 131
   savers 34, 98, 186, 194-195
   shots 147, 152
screens, virtual 123-125
scripts 46
scroll bars 95
scrolling screens 124-125
selecting a printer port 74
selecting files in File Manager 7, 10
sending faxes 170
serial port 81, 106, 176
service bureaus 73
setting alarms 166
setting startup directory 20
setting up your applications 115
setting up your desktop 5
Settings dialog 41
Setup program 58, 115, 143
setup errors 114
shareware 25, 45, 56, 57, 161, 167, 197
shell= 142

shells 12, 16, 25, 35, 127, 178, 141-145
shortcut keys, *see* keyboard shortcuts
simulating a hard disk 112
sizing windows 13
slow hard disks 105
SMARTDrive 49, 52, 107, 109, 112
soft fonts 62, 63, 64
Solitaire 106, 120-121, 142, 186, 191
Sound Blaster 183, 184
Sound Booster 183
sound cards 183
sounds, adding 179, 183-185, 198
specifying screen coordinates 20
speech synthesis 185
speeding up DOS applications 39, 40
speeding up printing 80, 84-87
speeding up your computer 99, 107-112
splitting a window in File Manager 10
spooling 50, 86, 87, 130
spreadsheets 3, 33, 88, 125, 129
Stacker 105, 182
standard mode 68, 107, 111
starting applications, *see* launching applications
starting utilities 50
starting Windows 17, 135
startup
   applications 130, 131
   directory, setting 20
   options 46, 47
   position 20
   screen, changing 127
   size 20
   StartUp group 14, 17, 27, 35
storing graphic images 162
streamlining applications 95
subdividing the screen 123
super VGA monitors 122
supercharging Windows 91
SuperPrint 62, 87
SuperQueue 84, 87
swap file 107, 108
swapping to disk 94
switches, command-line 39

switching
   applications 123
   printers 75
   drive icons 6
   drives in File Manager 6, 10
   options 39
   screens 124
   windows 25
   windows in File Manager 6
Symantec 56
system
   crashes 55
   files 133
   menu 22, 35, 41
   resources 48-53, 89-126, 139-140
System Editor 30, 76, 128, 132, 133, 160, 161
SYSTEM.INI 12, 128-133, 142

## T

Tab key 120-121
tabloid extra size 77
Talking Clock 166
tape drive 116
Task List 177, 178
Task Manager 5, 21, 33, 142, 146
telecommunications 160, 167, 168, 169
Telix 167
TEMP directory 101, 112
temporary files, deleting 101
term papers 88
Terminal 101, 130, 160, 167
TETRIS 192
text editors 12, 15, 18, 29-30, 31, 101, 109, 132, 160, 161, 175
text-only format 15, 84
things not to do in Windows 54, 55, 56, 105
tiling 6, 21
tints 83
tips on using DOS 54
titling an icon 43
Tom and Ed's Bogus Software 195
ToolBook 163
Tools Technologies 125
trackballs 106
TrackMan Portable 106
transferring files 176

**205**

# INDEX

transmitting data  168
Traveling Software  173, 176
TriPeaks  192
troubleshooting  98, 113-117
TrueType fonts  62
TSR programs, see
  memory-resident
  utilities
tuning SMARTDrive  109
Tut's Tomb  192
Type Manager  62
typefaces  87
typesetting  73, 78

## U

undeleting files  55, 56
unloading utilities  50
unrecoverable applica-
  tion errors  113, 114, 184
upper memory blocks  48,
  52-53
user interface hardware  118
using a mouse  10-11, 106
using a PIF editor  37
using batch files  31
using CHKDSK  49
*Using Computer Bulletin
  Boards*  169
using DOS applications  37-59
using generic PIF settings  39
using macros  20, 24
using parameters  44-47
using Program Manager  4

## V

Ventura Publisher  29, 77, 83
VGA monitors  122
VGALOGO.LGO  136
video display  122
video modes  39
View menu  10
viewing file properties  6
Virtual 386 Write Protect
  Device  56
virtual desktop  178
virtual machines  111, 123
virtual memory  108
Virtual Monitors  124
virtual screens  118, 123-125
viruses  56
volatile memory  112

## W

wallpaper  90, 101, 125
wallpaper, changing  127
wallpaper, removing  93, 134,
  139-140
wasting memory  51, 52
Whiskers  119
WideAngle  124, 178
Wilson WindowWare  161
WIN command  17
WIN.CNF  136
WIN.COM  136
WIN.INI  15-16, 18-19, 27, 28,
  31, 57, 64, 71, 72, 76, 127,
  128-133, 143, 147-152
WinComm  167
WinConnect  173, 176
window position  20, 22
window size  20, 22
Window Title box  43
Windows
  applets  100, 130, 160, 167
  applications  5, 11, 36,
    186, 187-190
  brag screens  186, 187-190
  changing colors  147-152
  communications
    programs  160, 167,
  customizing  127-157,
    172-178
  directory  81, 101, 146
  downloading fonts
    when starting  72
  environment  130
  exiting  12, 22, 35, 55, 68
  Express, Windows  35
  fine-tuning  91, 98,
    107-112, 126, 139-140
  games  186, 191-192,
    196-197
  Help, Windows  100, 131
  installing  29
  launching  17, 50 111, 135
  logo  134
  macros  165
  menu  4
  problems with  113-117
  prompting for
    parameters  47
  reloading fonts  70
  restarting  12
  screen savers  186, 193,
    194-195
  Setup, Windows  58,
    115, 143

shell  12, 35, 141-145, 178
sound  166
standard mode  68, 107, 111
system resources  48-53,
  96, 100
things not to do  54, 55,
  56, 102
user interface  118, 141-145
using CHKDSK with  49
using with a mouse  119
using without a
  mouse  106
wallpaper  90, 93, 134,
  139-140
WinEdit  161
WinExit  32, 35
WinFish  186, 193, 194-195
WINHELP.EXE  100
*Winning!*  192
WINPLACE command  20
WinPSX  72
WinSaver  22
WINUNZIP  182
Wired for Sound  166, 179,
  184, 185
Word 5.0  46, 50, 107
Word for Windows  15, 83,
  95, 100, 107, 123, 125,
  142, 161, 170, 176, 189-190
word processors  15, 33, 46,
  95, 100
WorkSets  22
Write  18, 101, 160

## X-Y-Z

Xerox  125
XyWrite  107, 176
Zenographics  62, 87, 146
Zeos keyboards  121
zoom level  22

# More from Peachpit Press...

**Corel Draw 2.0: Visual QuickStart Guide**
*Webster & Associates*
A visual tour of Corel Draw, including an interactive "Walkabout" tutorial disk. *(160 pages)*

**Desktop Publishing Secrets**
*Robert Eckhardt, Bob Weibel, and Ted Nace*
Hundreds of the best desktop publishing tips from 5 years of *Publish* magazine. *(550 pages)*

**The LaserJet Font Book**
*Katherine Pfeiffer*
A guide to LaserJet fonts and to using type effectively. Shows hundreds of LaserJet fonts from over a dozen vendors. *(320 pages)*

**LaserJet IIP Essentials**
*Steve Cummings, Mike Handa, and Jerold Whitmore*
Covers configuration and use of the IIP with word processing, database, spreadsheet, and desktop publishing programs. *(340 pages)*

**The Little DOS 5 Book**
*Kay Yarborough Nelson*
A quick and accessible guide to DOS 5. Includes numerous tips, tricks, and charts of keyboard shortcuts. *(160 pages)*

**The Little Laptop Book**
*Steve Cummings*
Provides information on using applications and utilities, printing on the road, and telecommunication. *(192 pages)*

**The Little Windows Book, 3.1 Edition**
*Kay Yarborough Nelson*
This second edition of Peachpit's popular book explains the subtle and not-so-subtle changes in version 3.1. *(144 pages)*

**The Little WordPerfect Book**
*Skye Lininger*
Gives step-by-step instructions for setting page margins, typing text, navigating with the cursor keys, and more. *(160 pages)*

**The Little WordPerfect for Windows Book**
*Kay Yarborough Nelson*
A quick and accessible guide to WordPerfect for Windows. Includes numerous tips and charts of keyboard shortcuts. *(200 pages)*

**Mastering Corel Draw, 2nd Edition**
*Chris Dickman and Rick Altman*
Provides beginning lessons and advanced tips on using this remarkable drawing program for Windows. Includes disk. *(408 pages)*

**PageMaker 4: An Easy Desk Reference**
*Robin Williams*
A reference book that lets you look up how to do specific tasks with PageMaker 4.0. *(784 pages, available Spring 1992)*

**PageMaker 4: Visual QuickStart Guide**
*Webster and Associates*
Provides a highly visual introduction to desktop publishing in PageMaker 4.0 for the PC. *(176 pages)*

**The PC is not a typewriter**
*Robin Williams*
Explains the principles behind the techniques for professional typesetting and how they can be utilized on the desktop. *(96 pages)*

**Ventura Tips and Tricks, 3rd Edition**
*Ted Nace and Daniel Will-Harris*
Performance tips, advice on using Ventura utilities, useful tables and charts, and clear explanations. *(790 pages)*

**Winning! The Awesome & Amazing Book of Windows Game Tips, Traps, & Sneaky Tricks**
*John Hedtke*
This book provides rules and explanations for setting up, running, and mastering each game in the Microsoft Entertainment Packs. *(232 pages)*

**WordPerfect: Desktop Publishing in Style, 2nd Edition**
*Daniel Will-Harris*
Peachpit's popular guide to producing documents with WordPerfect 5.1 or 5.0. *(650 pages)*

**WordPerfect for Windows, Visual QuickStart Guide**
*Webster & Associates*
A visual tour of WordPerfect for Windows, including an interactive "Walkabout" tutorial disk. *(280 pages)*

# Order Form
**(800) 283-9444 or (510) 548-4393**
**(510) 548-5991 fax**

| # | Title | Price | Total |
|---|---|---|---|
| | 101 Windows Tips & Tricks | 12.95 | |
| | Corel Draw 2.0: Visual QuickStart Guide (with disk) | 24.95 | |
| | Desktop Publishing Secrets | 27.95 | |
| | The LaserJet Font Book | 24.95 | |
| | LaserJet IIP Essentials | 21.95 | |
| | The Little DOS 5 Book | 12.95 | |
| | The Little Windows Book, 3.1 Edition | 12.95 | |
| | The Little WordPerfect Book | 12.95 | |
| | The Little WordPerfect for Windows Book | 12.95 | |
| | Mastering Corel Draw, 2nd Edition (with disk) | 32.95 | |
| | PageMaker 4: An Easy Desk Reference (PC Edition) | 29.95 | |
| | PageMaker 4: Visual QuickStart Guide (PC Edition) | 12.95 | |
| | The PC is not a typewriter | 9.95 | |
| | Ventura Tips and Tricks, 3rd Edition | 27.95 | |
| | Winning! | 14.95 | |
| | WordPerfect: Desktop Publishing in Style, 2nd Edition | 23.95 | |
| | WordPerfect for Windows: Visual QuickStart Guide (w/disk) | 27.95 | |

Tax of 8.25% applies to California residents only.
UPS ground shipping: $4 for first item,
 $1 each additional.
UPS 2nd day air: $7 for first item, $2 each additional.
Air mail to Canada: $6 for first item, $4 each additional.
Air mail overseas: $14 each item.

| | | |
|---|---|---|
| Subtotal | | |
| 8.25% Tax (CA only) | | |
| Shipping | | |
| **TOTAL** | | |

| Name | |
|---|---|
| Company | |
| Address | |
| City | State | Zip |
| Phone | Fax |
| ❑ Check enclosed | ❑ Visa | ❑ MasterCard |
| Company purchase order # | |
| Credit card # | Expiration Date |

**Peachpit Press, Inc. • 2414 Sixth Street • Berkeley, CA • 94710**
Your satisfaction is guaranteed or your money will be cheerfully refunded!